Learn Python in 7 Days

Get up-and-running with Python

Mohit
Bhaskar N. Das

BIRMINGHAM - MUMBAI

Learn Python in 7 Days

First published: May 2017

Production reference: 1190517

Published by Packt Publishing Ltd.
Livery Place
35 Livery Street
Birmingham
B3 2PB, UK.
ISBN 978-1-78728-838-6

www.packtpub.com

Credits

Authors
Mohit
Bhaskar N. Das

Reviewer
Rejah Rehim

Commissioning Editor
Kunal Parikh

Acquisition Editor
Denim Pinto

Content Development Editor
Anurag Ghogre

Technical Editor
Hussain Kanchwala

Copy Editor
Muktikant Garimella

Project Coordinator
Ulhas Kambali

Proofreader
Safis Editing

Indexer
Pratik Shirodkar

Graphics
Abhinash Sahu

Production Coordinator
Deepika Naik

About the Authors

Mohit (rohitraj.cs@gmail.com) is a Python programmer with a keen interest in the field of information security. He has completed his bachelor's degree in technology in computer science from Kurukshetra University, Kurukshetra, and master's in engineering (2012) in computer science from Thapar University, Patiala. He is a C|EH, ECSA from EC-Council USA and a former IBMer. He currently works in Sapient. He has published several articles in national and international magazines. He is the author of *Python Penetration Testing Essentials* and *Python: Penetration Testing for Developers*, also by Packt.

His LinkedIn profile is https://www.linkedin.com/in/mohit-990a852a/.

First of all, I am grateful to the Almighty for helping me to complete this book. I would like to thank my mother for her love and encouraging support and my father for raising me in a house with desktops and laptops. A big thanks to the co-author, Bhaskar Das. I would also like to thank everyone who has contributed to the publication of this book, including the publisher, especially the technical reviewers and also the editors, Denim and Anurag. Last but not least, I'm grateful to my i7 Dell XPS laptop, without which it would not have been possible to write this book.

Bhaskar N. Das (bhaskarndas@gmail.com) is an application developer with a keen interest in the field of analytics and financial markets. He completed his Bachelor of Technology in Mechanical Engineering from Dehradun Institute of Technology, India and his master's degree in science (2014) in CSR and ethical management from FH BFI, Vienna, Austria. He has eight years of experience with IBM and has worked on several web and analytics-related technologies. He has published technical articles in leading magazines.

His LinkedIn profile is https://www.linkedin.com/in/bhaskar-das-093a2012/.

It has been my pleasure to work with the Packt team, and I am thankful to them for providing me with such a wonderful opportunity. I am also thankful to my co-author Mohit for his invaluable help. Finally, I am thankful to my family who just helped me to timely complete the work. Well, this work would not have been possible without the newly devised CDP tool, so a great thanks should be given to it and also to all the resources that helped in the timely completion of this book.

About the Reviewer

Rejah Rehim is currently a security architect with Faya Innovations, India and is a long-time preacher of open source and has authored a book titled, *Effective Python Penetration Testing*. He is a steady contributor to the Mozilla Foundation and his name has been featured in the San Francisco Monument made by the Mozilla Foundation.

He is a part of the Mozilla add-on review board and has contributed to the development of several node modules. He has also been credited with the creation of eight Mozilla add-ons, including the highly successful Clear Console add-on which was selected as one of the best Mozilla add-ons of 2013. With a user base of more than 44,000, it has registered more than 6,50,000 downloads till date. He has successfully created the world's first one-of-a-kind security testing browser bundle, PenQ, an open source Linux-based penetration testing browser bundle preconfigured with tools for spidering, advanced web searching, fingerprinting, and so on.

Rejah is also an active member of the OWASP and a chapter leader of OWASP Kerala. He is also an active speaker at Coffee@DBG, one of the most premier monthly tech rendezvous in Technopark, Kerala. Besides being a part of the Cyber Security division of Faya currently and QBurst in the past, Rejah is also a fan of process automation and has implemented it in Faya.

www.PacktPub.com

For support files and downloads related to your book, please visit www.PacktPub.com.

Did you know that Packt offers eBook versions of every book published, with PDF and ePub files available? You can upgrade to the eBook version at www.PacktPub.com and as a print book customer, you are entitled to a discount on the eBook copy. Get in touch with us at service@packtpub.com for more details.

At www.PacktPub.com, you can also read a collection of free technical articles, sign up for a range of free newsletters and receive exclusive discounts and offers on Packt books and eBooks.

https://www.packtpub.com/mapt

Get the most in-demand software skills with Mapt. Mapt gives you full access to all Packt books and video courses, as well as industry-leading tools to help you plan your personal development and advance your career.

Why subscribe?

- Fully searchable across every book published by Packt
- Copy and paste, print, and bookmark content
- On demand and accessible via a web browser

Customer Feedback

Thanks for purchasing this Packt book. At Packt, quality is at the heart of our editorial process. To help us improve, please leave us an honest review on this book's Amazon page at `https://www.amazon.com/Learn-Python-7-days-Mohit/dp/1787288382/`.

If you'd like to join our team of regular reviewers, you can e-mail us at customerreviews@packtpub.com. We award our regular reviewers with free eBooks and videos in exchange for their valuable feedback. Help us be relentless in improving our products!

Table of Contents

Preface

Python was initially developed by Guido Von Rossum as a fun project and was named after his favorite show Monty Python's Flying Circus. It was developed in 1991, but it started becoming popular around 2008. A major contributor to this popularity was Google, which has developed a number of platforms using Python. Recently, Python has been popularized by cloud, DevOps, data science, data analytics, machine learning, and natural language processing. With more and more data harvesting and data processing, people want to get into new types of job roles, which require basic programming skills, and Python perfectly suits all the categories of job work. *Learn Python in 7 Days* has been designed to give such people an easy way to learn and master the basics of Python in 7 days. The book covers the basic and necessary concepts that are required to understand the working of the Python language. The book is for all types of readers and learners. It also acts as a refresher for experienced people. We believe that we have covered as much as possible for making it a book to be finished in seven days; however, we believe that merely reading the book is not sufficient to master programming skills. It will take more than that to achieve mastery. We hope you enjoy reading the book and use it as a good learning book.

What this book covers

Chapter 1, *Getting Started with Python*, gives you the background of Python programming language, along with installation instructions and basic commands.

Chapter 2, *Type Variables and Operators*, gives you an idea of variable types and the various types of operators used in Python.

Chapter 3, *Strings*, sheds light on various strings and string operations in Python.

Chapter 4, *Lists*, gives the idea of one of the important collection types, called lists, available in Python and all the relevant operations that could be done on lists.

Chapter 5, *Dictionary*, covers another important collection type available in Python and deals with the basics of dictionary and the various operations on a dictionary.

Chapter 6, *Control Statements and Loops*, discusses about various control statements, such as if statement, and loops (for, while, and so on), which could be used to write a piece of code in Python.

Chapter 7, *Function and Scope of Variable*, gives you an idea about functions that could be user-defined or built in. The chapter talks about the basics of a function and various operations. Also, the chapter gives you an idea about the validity of a variable within the particular scope of the code block.

Chapter 8, *Modules and Packages*, discusses about various modules and packages that are available in Python and also how to create your own package and module.

Chapter 9, *File Handling and Exceptions*, is divided into two parts; the first part deals with different file handling operations and the second part deals with exception handling.

Chapter 10, *Collections*, gives you the primer for different types and subtypes of collections in Python and explains the basic operations that could be done on them.

Chapter 11, *Class and Objects*, finally gives you an idea about some object-oriented programming concepts that are available in Python.

What you need for this book

For this book, you need to install Python 2.7x version on your machine, along with a simple text editor (Notepad or Notepad++). All the examples are meant to be run on the Python 2.7 version and will not work in Python 3.x versions.

Who this book is for

This book is intended for people who have zero to some background in computer programming. It is also intended for people who want to have some refresher in Python programming.

Conventions

In this book, you will find a number of text styles that distinguish between different kinds of information. Here are some examples of these styles and an explanation of their meaning.

Code words in text, database table names, folder names, filenames, file extensions, pathnames, dummy URLs, user input, and Twitter handles are shown as follows: "The next step is to edit `build.properties` file."

A block of code is set as follows:

```
print "Name Marks Age"
print ( "%s %14.2f %11d" % ("John Doe", 80.67, 27))
print ( "%s %12.2f %11d" %("Bhaskar" ,76.901, 27))
print ( "%s %3.2f %11d" %("Mohit", 56.98, 25))
```

Any command-line input or output is written as follows:

```
$ brew install python
```

New terms and **important words** are shown in bold. Words that you see on the screen, for example, in menus or dialog boxes, appear in the text like this: "Once done, click on **Activate**."

Warnings or important notes appear in a box like this.

Tips and tricks appear like this.

Reader feedback

Feedback from our readers is always welcome. Let us know what you think about this book-what you liked or disliked. Reader feedback is important for us as it helps us develop titles that you will really get the most out of. To send us general feedback, simply e-mail feedback@packtpub.com, and mention the book's title in the subject of your message. If there is a topic that you have expertise in and you are interested in either writing or contributing to a book, see our author guide at www.packtpub.com/authors.

Customer support

Now that you are the proud owner of a Packt book, we have a number of things to help you to get the most from your purchase.

Downloading the example code

You can download the example code files for this book from your account at `https://gith ub.com/PacktPublishing/Learn-Python-in-7-days`. If you purchased this book elsewhere, you can visit `http://www.packtpub.com/support` and register to have the files e-mailed directly to you.

You can download the code files by following these steps:

1. Log in or register to our website using your e-mail address and password.
2. Hover the mouse pointer on the **SUPPORT** tab at the top.
3. Click on **Code Downloads & Errata**.
4. Enter the name of the book in the **Search** box.
5. Select the book for which you're looking to download the code files.
6. Choose from the drop-down menu where you purchased this book from.
7. Click on **Code Download**.

Once the file is downloaded, please make sure that you unzip or extract the folder using the latest version of:

- WinRAR / 7-Zip for Windows
- Zipeg / iZip / UnRarX for Mac
- 7-Zip / PeaZip for Linux

The code bundle for the book is also hosted on GitHub at https://github.com/PacktPublishing/Java-9-Programming-By_Example. We also have other code bundles from our rich catalog of books and videos available at `https://github.com/P acktPublishing/`. Check them out!

Errata

Although we have taken every care to ensure the accuracy of our content, mistakes do happen. If you find a mistake in one of our books-maybe a mistake in the text or the code-we would be grateful if you could report this to us. By doing so, you can save other readers from frustration and help us improve subsequent versions of this book. If you find any errata, please report them by visiting http://www.packtpub.com/submit-errata, selecting your book, clicking on the **Errata Submission Form** link, and entering the details of your errata. Once your errata are verified, your submission will be accepted and the errata will be uploaded to our website or added to any list of existing errata under the Errata section of that title.

To view the previously submitted errata, go to https://www.packtpub.com/books/content/support and enter the name of the book in the search field. The required information will appear under the **Errata** section.

Piracy

Piracy of copyrighted material on the Internet is an ongoing problem across all media. At Packt, we take the protection of our copyright and licenses very seriously. If you come across any illegal copies of our works in any form on the Internet, please provide us with the location address or website name immediately so that we can pursue a remedy.

Please contact us at copyright@packtpub.com with a link to the suspected pirated material.

We appreciate your help in protecting our authors and our ability to bring you valuable content.

Questions

If you have a problem with any aspect of this book, you can contact us at questions@packtpub.com, and we will do our best to address the problem.

1
Getting Started with Python

The Python language had a humble beginning in the late 1980s when a Dutchman Guido Von Rossum started working on a fun project, which would be a successor to ABC language with better exception handling and capability to interface with OS Amoeba at Centrum Wiskunde and Informatica. It first appeared in 1991. Python 2.0 was released in the year 2000 and Python 3.0 was released in the year 2008. The language was named Python after the famous British television comedy show Monty Python's Flying Circus, which was one of Guido's favorite television programmes. Here we will see why Python has suddenly influenced our lives and the various applications that use Python and its implementations. In this chapter, you will be learning the basic installation steps that are required to perform on different platforms (that is Windows, Linux, and Mac), about environment variables, setting up of environment variables, file formats, Python interactive shell, basic syntaxes and finally printing out formatted output.

Why Python?

Now you might be suddenly bogged with the question, why Python? According to Institute of Electrical and Electronics Engineers (IEEE) 2016 ranking Python ranked third after C and Java. As per Indeed.com's data of 2016, the Python job market search ranked fifth. Clearly, all the data points to the ever rising demand in the job market for Python. Its a cool language if you want to learn just for fun or if you want to build your career around Python, you will adore the language. At school level, many schools have started including Python programming for kids. With new technologies taking the market by surprise Python has been playing a dominant role. Whether it is cloud platform, mobile app development, BigData, IoT with Raspberry Pi, or the new Blockchain technology, Python is being seen as a niche language platform to develop and deliver a scalable and robust applications.

Some key features of the language are:

- Python programs can run on any platform, you can carry code created in Windows machine and run it on Mac or Linux
- Python has inbuilt large library with prebuilt and portable functionality, also known as the standard library
- Python is an expressive language
- Python is free and open source
- Python code is about one third of the size of equivalent C++ and Java code
- Python can be both dynamically and strongly typed--dynamically typed means it is a type of variable that is interpreted at runtime, which means, in Python, there is no need to define the type (`int` or `float`) of the variable

Python applications

One of the most famous platforms where Python is extensively used is YouTube. The other places where you will find Python being extensively used are the special effects in Hollywood movies, drug evolution and discovery, traffic control systems, ERP systems, cloud hosting, e-commerce platform, CRM systems, and whatever field you can think of.

Versions

At the time of writing this book, two main versions of the Python programming language were available in the market, which are Python 2.x and Python 3.x. The stable release as of writing the book were Python 2.7.13 and Python 3.6.0.

Implementations of Python

Major implementations include CPython, Jython, IronPython, MicroPython, and PyPy.

Installation

Here we will look forward to the installation of Python on three different OS platforms, namely, Windows, Linux, and Mac OS. Let's begin with the Windows platform.

Installation on Windows platform

Python 2.x can be downloaded from `https://www.python.org/downloads`. The installer is simple and easy to install. Perform the following steps to install the setup:

1. Once you click on setup installer, you will get a small window on your desktop screen as shown here; click on **Next**:

2. Provide a suitable installation folder to install Python. If you don't provide the installation folder, then the installer will automatically create an installation folder for you, as shown in the following screenshot. Click on **Next**:

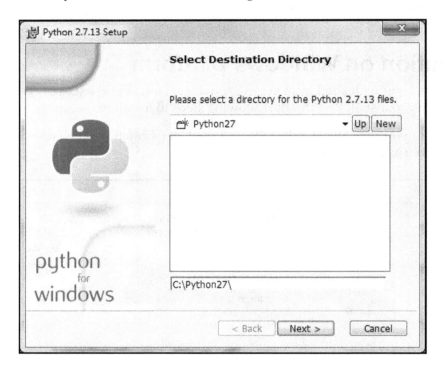

3. After completion of step 2, you will get a window to customize Python as shown in the preceding screenshot. Notice that the **Add python.exe to Path** option has been marked **x**. Select this option to add it to system path variable (which will be explained later in the chapter), and click on **Next**:

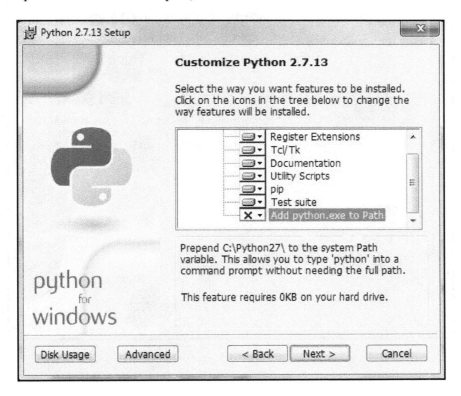

4. Finally, click on **Finish** to complete the installation:

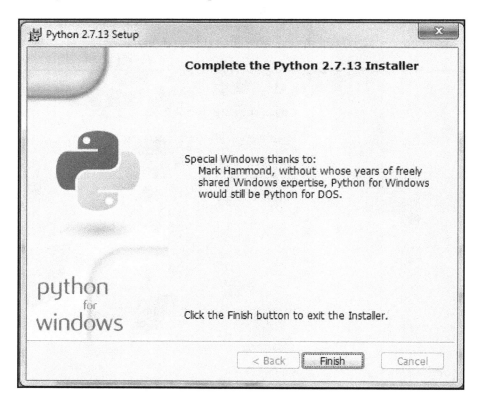

Installation on Linux platform

These days most of the Linux-based systems come preloaded with Python, so in most cases, you do not need to install it separately. However, if you do not find your desired version of Python on the Linux platform, you can download your desired version for a particular Linux platform from the site `https://www.python.org/downloads/source/`. Perform the following steps:

1. Extract the compressed file using the `tar -xvzf python_versionx.x` command.
2. Browse the directory of the compressed file as shown in the screenshot:

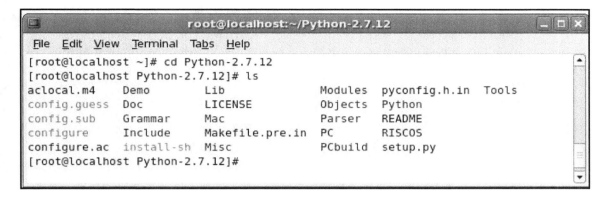

3. Run the following commands:

```
[root@localhost Python-2.7.12]# ./configure
[root@localhost Python-2.7.12]# make
[root@localhost Python-2.7.12]# make install
```

4. Use the command as shown in screenshot to ensure that Python is running:

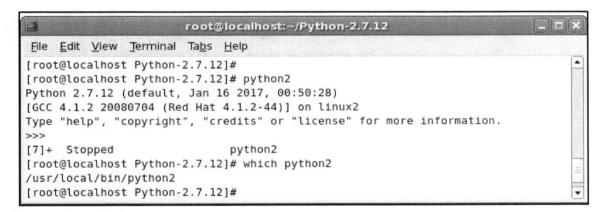

Installation on Mac OS

For Mac OS, you will get the installer from the site https://www.python.org/downloads/mac-osx/.

For the new Mac OS X, Sierra comes loaded with Python 2.7 and it's good for learning but the same cannot be used to develop advanced-level programs. You do not need to separately install Python on the new Mac OS X. However, a word of caution is that the version of Python packed with the Mac OS could be out of date and might require updating. If you still want to install a separate version, you can follow the simple steps mentioned as follows:

1. First of all, you might require to install Xcode, Xcode is the IDE for platform and can be downloaded from the Apple appstore.
2. Once Xcode is installed, you need to install the command-line tools, which can be installed by running the `xcode-select --install` command on the terminal found under `/Applications/Utilities/`, as shown in the following screenshot:

3. A pop-up window appears with three different options as shown here:

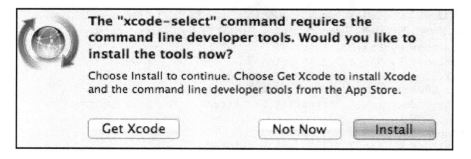

4. Once you click on **Install** and agree to their terms and conditions, the command-line tools will start to download and will be installed in few minutes depending on the Internet connection.

5. The next step in the process would be to install Homebrew, which is a package manager for Mac OS and handles the Python package. In order to install Homebrew, simply provide the following inputs to the terminal:

```
/usr/bin/ruby -e "$(curl -fsSL
https://raw.githubusercontent.com/Homebrew/install/master/install)"
```

6. To install the latest `python2` version, simply type `brew install python` on the terminal:

```
$ brew install python
```

In order to install `python3`, you need to use `brew install python3`.

Notepad++ installation

Notepad++ is one of the easy-to-use text editors and is a free open source software program, which could be easily downloaded from `https://notepad-plus-plus.org/`. We will be using this text editor to create simple programs.

Python file formats

Every language understands a file format, for example, like the C language file extension is `.c` likewise java language has a file extension `.java`. The Python file extension is `.py` while bytecode file extension is `.pyc`.

Python interactive shell

Python interactive shell is also known as **Integrated Development Environment (IDLE)**. With the Python installer, two interactive shells are provided: one is IDLE (Python GUI) and the other is Python (command line). Both can be used for running simple programs.

For complex programs and executing large files, the windows command prompt is used, where after the system variables are set automatically, large files are recognized and executed by the system.

```
Python 2.7.13 Shell

File  Edit  Shell  Debug  Options  Window  Help
Python 2.7.13 (v2.7.13:a06454b1afa1, Dec 17 2016, 20:42:59) [MSC v.1500 32 bit (Intel)] on win32
Type "copyright", "credits" or "license()" for more information.
>>> a=10
>>> b=4
>>> c=a+b
>>> print c
14
>>>
                                                                              Ln: 8  Col: 4
```

The preceding screenshot is what we call Python IDLE, which comes bundled with the Python installation. The next screenshot is of the command line that also comes bundled with the Python installation, or we can simply launch the Python command through the windows command line and get Python command line. For most of our programming instructions, we will be using the Python command line:

```
C:\Python27\python.exe

Python 2.7.13 (v2.7.13:a06454b1afa1, Dec 17 2016, 20:42:59) [MSC v.1500 32 bit (
Intel)] on win32
Type "help", "copyright", "credits" or "license" for more information.
>>> a=10
>>> b=4
>>> c=a+b
>>> print c
14
>>>
```

System or environment variables

If you remember the installation steps explained earlier, you might be still thinking what are system variables? They are a set of predefined variables, which are available to all programming units. If it's not set, then each and every time you want to run your program or execute a Python file, you will have to manually provide path for each Python executable, but if `python.exe` is set as a system variable, then the system automatically recognizes your programming instruction and starts executing.

Setting environment variables in Windows

Here, if `python.exe` is not provided to the path variable, then the system does not recognize `python` as a command, as shown in the following screenshot:

The Windows command prompt does not recognize `python` as shown in the previous screenshot. Once Python has been updated in the path variables or system variables, the windows command line recognizes the `python` command and executes as shown here:

During installation, the installer provides an option to set system variables, which we have seen in our installation steps. But in case you missed that out, you need not worry. You can manually set the system variables. Simply follow these steps:

1. Just right-click on **My Computer (older version of Windows PC)** or Computer (win 7 onwards) and select **Properties**. Once you have selected the properties, you will get the following screenshot where you need to select **Advanced system settings**:

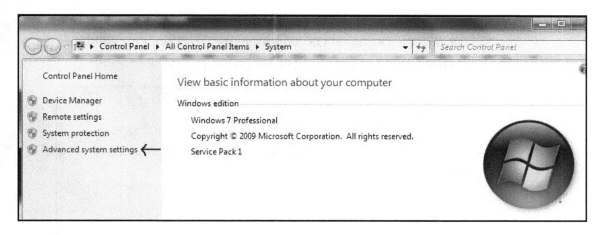

2. After you have clicked on **Advanced system settings**, you will get **System Properties**. Click on the **Environment Variables** button.

3. After completing Step 2, a window will pop up. From the **System variables** pane, select **Path** and click on the **Edit** button.

4. Your Python installation will look something like the following screenshot, where you need to right-click on the address bar and select the **Copy address as text** option:

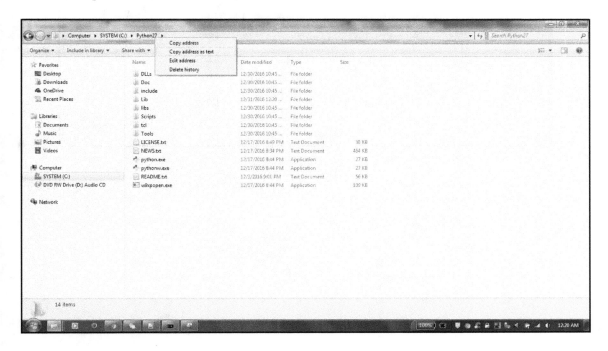

5. Add the Python installation folder path to the **Path** variable.
6. Click on **OK** and then again on **OK** to close all the windows. Our system variable is set:

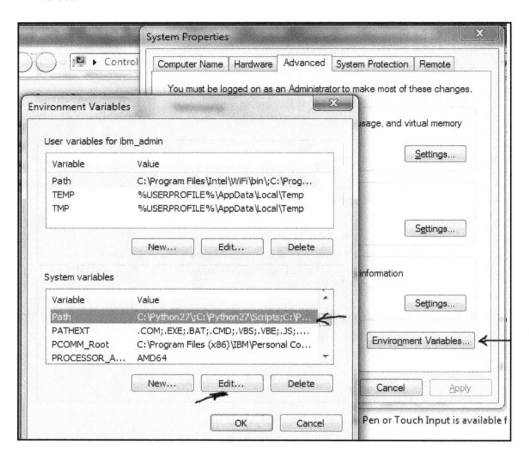

Setting environment variables in Linux

Linux comes with different types of shells and the Python directory path is usually `/usr/local/bin/python`:

- **csh shell**: Open the terminal and enter `setenv PATH "$PATH:/usr/local/bin/python"` followed by pressing *Enter*
- **bash shell**: On the terminal, enter `export PATH="$PATH:/usr/local/bin/python"` followed by pressing *Enter*
- **sh or ksh shell**: Enter `PATH="$PATH:/usr/local/bin/python"` followed by pressing *Enter*

Setting environment variables in Mac OS (OS 10.9)

Here, simply you need to edit the `launchd.conf` file and add the path variable to the file:

```
$ sudo edit /etc/launchd.conf
setenv PYTHONPATH /Users/vesper/temp:/Users/vesper/misc
```

Writing a simple Hello World! program

Congratulations on your successful installation. Now you can start programming. Open Notepad++ and create a new file. In the new file, type the following:

```
print "Hello World!"
```

Save the file as `hello.py`.

Open the command prompt and traverse to the folder where your file is located using `cd` and then the path of the folder. For executing the file, the command will be `python hello.py` as shown in the following screenshot:

It is quite easy, isn't it? Likewise, you can execute all the Python files. Once you start working on projects and large files, it's always good to remain organized by creating a folder structure.

Basic Python syntax

Basic syntaxes can be referred to as simple guidelines that every programming language requires. Let's try to understand from our daily lives. Let's say you can't eat your food without having it dressed and placed properly on the platter. You need to have proper dressing of food before you can consume it. You prepare a special drink comprising three measures of Gordon gin, one of vodka, half of Kina Lillet, and follow the process to mix in steps. The process is necessary to have a perfect blend. These are sort of syntaxes when we talk in terms of programming languages.

Kina Lillet-Lillet (French pronunciation: [li'le]), classed as an aromatized wine within EU law, is a French aperitif wine from Podensac, a small village south of Bordeaux. It is a blend of 85% Bordeaux region wines (Semillon for the Blanc and for the Rosé, Merlot for the Rouge) and 15% macerated liqueurs, mostly citrus liqueurs (peels of sweet oranges from Spain and Morocco and peels of bitter green oranges from Haiti). The mix is then stirred in oak vats until blended. During the aging process, Lillet is handled as a Bordeaux wine (undergoing fining, racking, filtering, and so on).

The preceding information has been taken from `https://en.wikipedia.org/wiki/Lillet`.

Comments in Python

In Python, there are two types of comments--one is a single-line comment and the other is multiline comment. For a single-line comment, # is used, while for a multiline comment, triple quotes " " " are used:

```
#This is a single line comment in Python

print "Hello World" #This is a single comment in Python

""" For multi-line
comment use three
double quotes
...
"""
print "Hello World!"
```

Triple, double and single quotes

Python doesn't care if you use single quotes or double quotes to print a single statement. But, surely, both has some significance while printing complex statements, which we will see soon.

`print "Hello World!"` and `print 'Hello World!'` will give the same output `Hello World!` two times:

How will you print something like this:

I am mad in love do you think I am doing the right thing? One way is to enclose the complete thing within the triple quotes as shown here:

```
print '''I am mad in love
                do you think
                        I am doing
                                the right thing '''
```

Alternatively, you can also use double quotes three times to achieve the same thing:

```
print """I am mad in love
                do you think
                        I am doing

                                the right thing """
```

The preceding two examples are not in formatted form, they are just to show how we can achieve multiline printing.

Let's try another example. What should be the outcome of the following statement?

```
print 'Hey there it's a cow'
```

The preceding piece of code gives the following results:

```
C:pydev>python hello.py
File "hello.py", line 1
print 'Hey there it's a cow'
            ^
SyntaxError: invalid syntax
```

Python simply interprets that the statement terminated with a single quote after it. The solution is to enclose the complete sentence within double quotes as shown:

```
print "Hey there it's a cow"
```

Adding double quotes (") gives an error-free output as shown:

```
C:pydev>python hello.py
Hey there it's a cow
```

Python back slash

The Python back slash is used for continuation of the `print` statement. You can stretch a single statement across multiple lines:

```
print "Hello
    world "
```

This gives the following output:

```
C:pydev>python hello.py
Hello world
```

String inside the quotes

For printing a string, either a pair of single (' ') quotes or pair of double quotes (" ") can be used as shown in the succeeding examples:

```
print "Hello World 'Mr' Bond"
print 'old world "but" still good'
```

This gives the following results:

```
C:pydev>python hello.py
Hello World 'Mr' Bond
old world "but" still good
```

Escape sequence in Python

The escape sequence is used to insert the tab, the newline, the backspace, and other special characters into your code. They give you greater control and flexibility to format your statements and code:

Escape	Sequence Meaning
b	Backspace
a	Sound system bell
n	Newline
t	Horizontal tab
	The character
'	Single quotation mark
"	Double quotation mark

```
print 'a'
print 'tHermit'
print "i know , they are 'great'"
```

The output is as follows:

```
C:pydev>python hello.py
Hermit
i know , they are 'great'
```

The preceding code executes with a beep sound. If you did not hear the beep sound, check your speakers.

String concatenation

Two strings can be joined using the + operator:

```
print "Only way to join" + "two strings"
```

The following is the output of the preceding code:

```
C:pydev>python string_concatenation.py
Only way to join two strings
```

Formatted output

Consider an example where you would want to print the name, marks, and the age of the person:

```
print "Name", "Marks", "Age"
print "John Doe", 80.67, "27"
print "Bhaskar", 76.908, "27"
print "Mohit", 56.98, "25"
```

The output will be as follows:

```
C:pydev>python hello.py
Name Marks Age
John Doe 80.67 27
Bhaskar 76.908 27
Mohit 56.98 25
```

You can see the output, but the output that is displayed is not formatted. Python allows you to set the formatted output. If you have done some coding in C language, then you should be familiar with %d, %f, %s. In order to represent an integer %d is used, %f is used for float, and %s is used for string. If you used %5d, it means 5 spaces. If you used %5.2f, it means 5 spaces and .2 means precision. The decimal part of the number or the precision is set to 2. Let's use the formatting on the preceding example:

```
print "Name Marks Age"
print ( "%s %14.2f %11d" % ("John Doe", 80.67, 27))
print ( "%s %12.2f %11d" %("Bhaskar" ,76.901, 27))
print ( "%s %3.2f %11d" %("Mohit", 56.98, 25))
```

The output we get is as follows:

```
C:pydev>python hello.py
Name Marks Age
John Doe 80.67 27
Bhaskar 76.90 27
Mohit 56.98 25
```

The preceding output is much better than the previous one. You can see `Marks 76.901` set to `76.90` automatically.

Indentation

The most unique characteristic of Python, unlike other programming languages, is indentation. Indentation not only makes Python code readable, but also distinguishes each block of code from the other. Let's explain this with an example:

```
def fun():
    pass
for each in "Australia":
    pass
```

While writing the code, a new block of code starts with a colon followed by a tab. Here, after the function `fun()`, a colon is provided which will start the function body, `pass` is part of the function `fun()` and it is placed at one tab space. Likewise, the for loop starts with a colon. Here, most people get confused whether to use a tab or space. It is advisable to stick to only one type and follow the same across the whole code. If the indentation is not strictly implemented, then code execution will throw an error.

Summary

So far, we did a walkthrough of the beginning and the brief history of Python. We looked through various implementations and flavors of Python. We also learned about installation on various platforms. We learned about basic syntaxes that are used in writing the code and also we learned about various escape sequences that would make writing the code simple. We finally learned about the importance of indentation in Python.

In the next chapter, we will see immutable data types.

2
Type Variables and Operators

In the last chapter, you learned a little bit about the history of Python. You learned the steps to install Python and some basic syntax of the language. In the basic syntax, you learned about types of comments that can be used in the code, various types of quotes, escape sequence that can be handy, and finally, you learned about the formatting of strings. In this chapter, you will learn about assignment statements, arithmetic operators, comparison operators, assignment operators, bitwise operators, logical operators, membership operators, and identity operators.

Variables

So, what is a variable? Consider that your house needs a name. You place a nameplate at the front gate of your house. People will now recognize your house through that nameplate. That nameplate can be considered as variable. Like a nameplate points to the house, a variable points to the value that is stored in memory. When you create a variable, the interpreter will reserve some space in the memory to store values. Depending on the data type of the variable, the interpreter allocates memory and makes a decision to store a particular data type in the reserved memory. Various data types, such as integers, decimals, or characters, can be stored by assigning different data types to the variables. Python variables are usually dynamically typed, that is, the type of the variable is interpreted during runtime and you need not specifically provide a type to the variable name, unlike what other programming languages require. There are certain rules or naming conventions for naming variables. The following are the rules:

- Reserved key words such as `if`, `else`, and so on cannot be used for naming variables

- Variable names can begin with _, $, or a letter
- Variable names can be in lower case and uppercase
- Variable names cannot start with a number
- White space characters are not allowed in the naming of a variable

You can assign values to the variable using = or assignment operator.

Syntax:

```
<variable name>= < expression >
```

Single assignment

Here, we will illustrate the use of the assignment operator (=) with an example:

```
city='London' # A string variable assignment.
money = 100.75 # A floating point number assignment
count=4 #An integer assignment
```

In this case, we assigned three different values to three variables using the = operator.

Multiple assignment

A single value can be assigned to several variables simultaneously. For example:

```
a = b = c = 1
```

Data types in Python

What is a data type in any programming language? Let's try to understand with a real life problem. We use water, oil, liquid soap, syrups, and so on in our day to day life. How do you categorize these items? Let's take another set of examples of bar soap, cell phone, and so on; what classification would you like to give these items? Answer to all these questions is simple: solid, liquid, and gases. Yes, we have these three broader classifications for any item that we have heard about or used in our day to day life. Same is the case in the programming world. Each and every thing needs to be categorized under different types. There are many types of data, such as numbers, strings, character, images, and so on.

Data types can be broadly categorized into five different types, listed as follows:

- Numbers
- String
- Tuples
- List
- Dictionary

Numeric data types or numbers

There are generally four numeric data types in Python. They are integers, long integers, floating point numbers, and complex numbers.

Integers and long integers

Integers include zero, all of the positive whole numbers, and all of the negative whole numbers. The interpreter first checks the expression on the right hand side of the assignment operator and then binds the value with its variable name; this process is termed as variable definition or initialization. The int or integer data type ranges from -2^{31} to $(2^{31}-1)$; the leading minus sign shows the negative values. Beyond these ranges, the interpreter will add L to indicate a long integer, as shown in the following screenshot:

```
C:\windows\system32\cmd.exe - python

C:\>python
Python 2.7.13 (v2.7.13:a06454b1afa1, Dec 17 2016, 20:42:59) [MSC v.1500 32 bit (
Intel)] on win32
Type "help", "copyright", "credits" or "license" for more information.
>>> 214768979765
214768979765L
>>> 263547877864*1000
263547877864000L
>>>
```

Floating point numbers

Numbers with certain places after the decimal point are referred to as floating point numbers in the programming language:

- The floating point number type ranges approximately from -10 to 10^{308} and has 16 digits of precision.
- There are two ways to write a floating point number. It can be written using ordinary decimal notation or scientific notation. Scientific notation is often useful for mentioning very large numbers, as shown in the following screenshot:

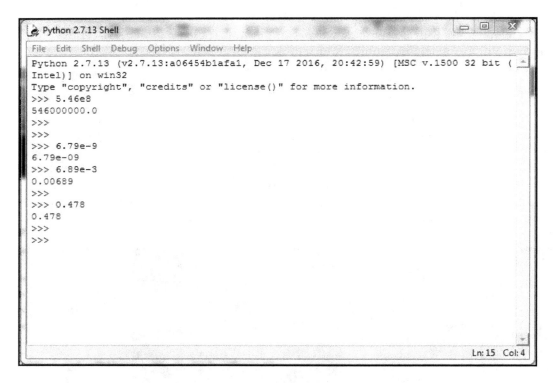

Complex numbers

A complex number has both real and imaginary parts, and Python allows you to specify this data type in a very easy and convenient way.

Syntax:

```
<variable name>=complex(x,y)
```

OR

```
<variable name>=x+yj
```

Here, x is the real part and y is the imaginary part. Here, j plays the role of iota.

It will be clearer with the following screenshot:

Here, we declare two variables to denote complex numbers. One way to achieve is to use `complex()` method and the other way is to use the standard notation as used in mathematics.

In standard complex number notation, *x+ij*, *i* is used to denote the starting of the imaginary part and stands for iota. *j* denotes the imaginary part. The credit for conceiving the idea of complex numbers goes to Italian mathematician Gerolamo Cardano in 1545.

Source: `https://en.wikipedia.org/wiki/Complex_number`

Boolean data type

A Boolean data type generally has only two values `'True'` or `'False'`. Boolean data type is a sub type of integers.

Syntax:

```
<variable name>=<'True' or 'False'>
```

Boolean data types can be referred to as an on and off switch, which has only two values to chose from:

```
C:\windows\system32\cmd.exe - python

C:\>python
Python 2.7.13 (v2.7.13:a06454b1afa1, Dec 17 2016, 20:42:59) [MSC v.1500 32 bit (
Intel)] on win32
Type "help", "copyright", "credits" or "license" for more information.
>>>
>>>
>>> x=3
>>>
>>> y=3
>>>
>>> x<y
False
>>>
>>> x==y
True
>>>
>>>
```

In the preceding example, we try to compare the value of x with the value of y, and when we use the == operator, the value of the Boolean is returned as True.

String data types

A Python string is a contiguous sequence of Unicode characters. Single quotes or double quotes can be used to denote a string, as we saw in Chapter 1, *Getting Started with Python*. For multiline string representation, ''' or """ can be used.

Syntax:

```
<variable name>= <String sequence>
```

You will understand better with the following screenshot:

More details on strings, tuples, list, and dictionary will be covered in the coming chapters.

American Standard Code for Information Interchange (ASCII) character sets

The succeeding table shows the mapping of the first 128 ASCII codes to character values. The left column digits are the leftmost digits of the ASCII code. The top row's digits represent the rightmost digits. For example, the ASCII code of character *A* would be *65*.

	0	1	2	3	4	5	6	7	8	9
0	NUL	SOH	STX	ETX	EOT	ENQ	ACK	BEL	BS	HT
1	LF	VT	FF	CR	SO	SI	DLE	DCI	DC2	DC3
2	DC4	NAK	SYN	ETB	CAN	EM	SUB	ESC	FS	GS
3	RS	US	SP	!	"	#	$	%	&	`
4	(	)	*	+	,	-	.	/	0	1
5	2	3	4	5	6	7	8	9	:	;
6	<	=	>	?	@	A	B	C	D	E
7	F	G	H	I	J	K	L	M	N	O
8	P	Q	R	S	T	U	V	W	X	Y
9	Z	[		]	^	_	'	a	b	c
10	d	e	f	g	h	i	j	k	l	m
11	n	o	p	q	r	s	t	u	v	w
12	x	y	z	{			}	~	DEL		

ASCII was developed primarily for telegraph code. Bell labs brought out 7-bit teleprinter code for commercial promotion and official work on the ASCII code began on October 6, 1960.
Source: https://en.wikipedia.org/wiki/ASCII

Conversion functions

In order to convert a character value to ASCII code, the `ord()` function is used, and for converting ASCII code to character, the `chr()` function is used, as shown in the following screenshot:

Here, when we want to get the ASCII code for `'A'`, it shows 65, which you can easily get from the aforementioned table. The letter `'A'` can be located on the sixth row and fifth column; thus, its value is 65. Likewise, we can get the letter corresponding to a particular ASCII code.

Arithmetic expressions

Arithmetic expressions in any language comprise operands and operators. For reference, *x* and *y* are used as operands having values *10* and *20*, respectively. The following table shows the precedence order:

Operator	Description
**	**Exponent**: Performs exponential (power) calculations on operators
*	**Multiplication**: Multiplies values on either side of the operator
/	**Division**: Divides the left-hand operand by the right-hand operand
%	**Modulus**: Divides the left-hand operand by the right-hand operand and returns the remainder
+	**Addition**: Adds values on either side of the operator
−	**Subtraction**: Subtracts the right-hand operand from the left-hand operand

In an arithmetic expression, generally, the rule of **Bracket, Of, Division, Multiplication, Addition, and Subtraction (BODMAS)** is followed, and operators have their own precedence order. Exponentiation enjoys a higher precedence order, while addition and subtraction have a lower precedence order.

The decreasing precedence order is as follows:

- Exponent
- Unary negation
- Multiplication, division, modulus
- Addition, subtraction

If operands are of the same data type, then the resulting value is also of that type. However, addition of two `int` data types can produce a `long` integer.

Mixed mode arithmetic

The arithmetic operation involving both integer and floating point numbers is called **mixed mode arithmetic**. When each operand is of a different data type, the resulting value is of the more general type, and `float` is the more general type.

The following screenshot will make it clearer for you:

Mixed Mode Conversion

In the preceding example, `11/2.0`, the less general type integer, `11`, is temporarily and automatically converted into float `11.0`. Then, the calculation is performed. It is called **mixed mode conversion**.

Type conversions

It is easy to convert the data type of operands using a type conversion function. Let's understand with some examples:

```
C:\windows\system32\cmd.exe - python

C:\>python
Python 2.7.13 (v2.7.13:a06454b1afa1, Dec 17 2016, 20:42:59) [MSC v.1500 32 bit (
Intel)] on win32
Type "help", "copyright", "credits" or "license" for more information.
>>>
>>>
>>> int(4.77)
4
>>>
>>> long(65)
65L
>>>
>>> float(68)
68.0
>>>
>>> str(98)
'98'
>>>
>>>
```

In the preceding screenshot, 4.77 is converted into 4. In order to convert 4.77 into the int data type, the int() function is used. Likewise, if you want to convert into float, use the float() function.

Operators

Python supports the following types of operators:

- Arithmetic operators.
- Comparison operators
- Assignment operators
- Bitwise operators
- Logical operators
- Membership operators
- Identity operators

Arithmetic operators

Arithmetic expressions comprise operands and operators:

Operator	Description
**	**Exponent**: Performs exponential (power) calculations on operands
*	**Multiplication**: Performs multiplication between operands
/	**Division**: Performs division between operands
%	**Modulus**: Performs modulus division between operands
+	**Addition**: Performs addition between operands
−	**Subtraction**: Performs subtraction between operands

We have already discussed the precedence order of the operators.

Comparison operators

Like any other language, Python also supports comparison operators. Comparison operators return True or False:

Operator	Description
==	Checks the equality
<	Returns True if the left-hand side operand is less than the right-hand side operand
>	Returns True if the left-hand side operand is greater than the right-hand side operand
<=	Returns True if the left-hand side operand is less than or equal to the right-hand side operand
>=	Returns True if the left-hand side operand is greater than or equal to the right-hand side operand
!=	Returns True if the left-hand side operand is not equal to the right-hand side operand
<>	Returns True if the left-hand side operand is not equal to the right-hand side operand

Some examples of comparison operators and their outcome are shown in the following screenshot:

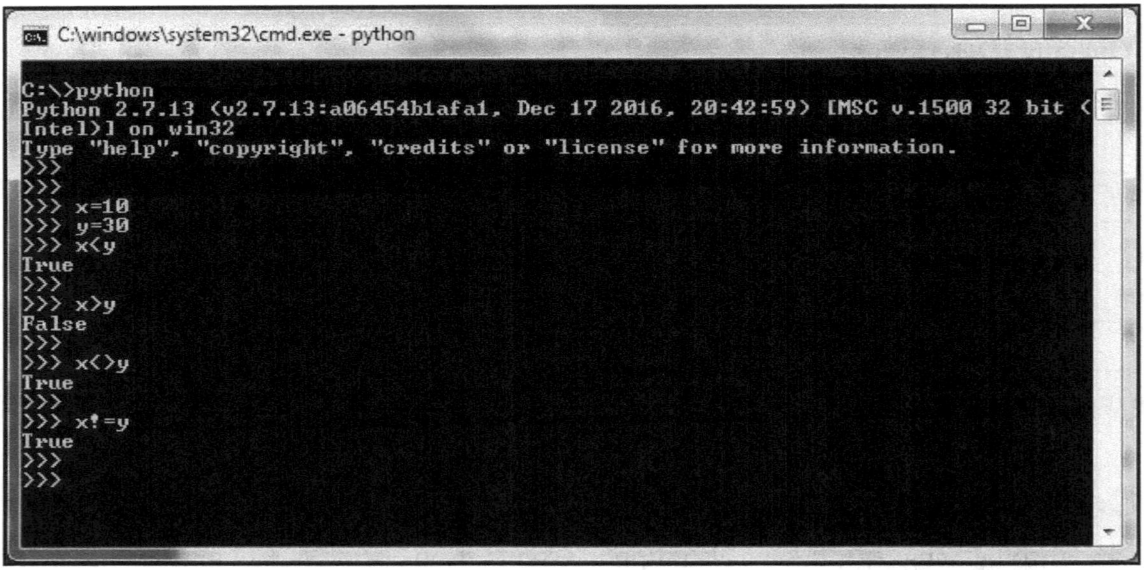

```
C:\windows\system32\cmd.exe - python

C:\>python
Python 2.7.13 (v2.7.13:a06454b1afa1, Dec 17 2016, 20:42:59) [MSC v.1500 32 bit (
Intel)] on win32
Type "help", "copyright", "credits" or "license" for more information.
>>>
>>>
>>> x=10
>>> y=30
>>> x<y
True
>>>
>>> x>y
False
>>>
>>> x<>y
True
>>>
>>> x!=y
True
>>>
>>>
```

Let's evaluate the following expression:

```
a < b < = c is equivalent to a<b and b<=c
```

Here, the and operator is used, b is evaluated only once, and c will not be evaluated if a < b is found False:

```
C:\windows\system32\cmd.exe - python

C:\>python
Python 2.7.13 (v2.7.13:a06454b1afa1, Dec 17 2016, 20:42:59) [MSC v.1500 32 bit (
Intel)] on win32
Type "help", "copyright", "credits" or "license" for more information.
>>> 12<5<John
False
>>>
>>> John>5>12
Traceback (most recent call last):
  File "<stdin>", line 1, in <module>
NameError: name 'John' is not defined
>>>
```

In the preceding example, 12<5 is evaluated first; if it is False, then the next expression will not be evaluated. If the operands are of different types, then they are converted to a common type. Otherwise, the == and != operators always consider objects of different types to be unequal.

Let's look at two different scenarios where we try to evaluate a float data type with an int data type, as shown:

Here, the operator evaluates to True in both the cases, as the interpreter converts one data type to another and then compares both the values.

Comparison between different data types:

- Numbers are compared arithmetically
- Strings are compared as per the alphabetical order, using the numeric equivalents
- Tuples and lists are compared according to the alphabetical order using the comparison of corresponding elements, which we will see in the coming chapters

Variants of assignment operator

Earlier in the chapter, you learned about the assignment operator, =. Now, we will see some more variants of the assignment operator, often used in combination with arithmetic operators:

Operator	Description
=	x=y , y is assigned to x

+=	x+=y is equivalent to x=x+y
-=	x-=y is equivalent to x=x-y
*=	x*=y is equivalent to x=x*y
/=	x/=y is equivalent to x=x/y
**=	x**=y is equivalent to x=x**y

Here, we will look at a few examples of the variants of the assignment operator:

Bitwise operators

Python supports bitwise operations. You might have come across *AND*, *OR*, or complementary operations:

Operator	Description
|	Performs binary *OR* operation
&	Performs binary *AND* operation
~	Performs binary *XOR* operation

^	Performs binary one's complement operation
<<	**Left shift operator**: The left-hand side operand bit is moved left by the number specified on the right-hand side
>>	**Right shift operator**: The left-hand side operand bit is moved right by the number specified on the right-hand side

The following screenshot illustrates the various usages of bitwise operators:

```
C:\windows\system32\cmd.exe - python

C:\>python
Python 2.7.13 (v2.7.13:a06454b1afa1, Dec 17 2016, 20:42:59) [MSC v.1500 32 bit (
Intel)] on win32
Type "help", "copyright", "credits" or "license" for more information.
>>>
>>> x=240
>>> y=1
>>> x|y
241
>>> x&y
0
>>> x^y
241
>>>
>>> x<<2
960
>>>
>>> x>>2
60
>>>
>>> ~x
-241
>>>
>>>
```

~x will give −241, which is in *2's complement* form due to a signed binary number.

Logical operators

Python supports logical operators *AND, OR,* and *NOT*:

Operator	Description
and	Returns True if both the right-hand and left-hand sides of the operator are true
or	Returns True if any side, either the right-hand side or the left-hand side, of the operator is true
not	If condition in the not operator is True, the not operator makes it False

These only evaluate their second argument if needed for their outcome, as shown in the following screenshot:

```
C:\windows\system32\cmd.exe - python

C:\>python
Python 2.7.13 (v2.7.13:a06454b1afa1, Dec 17 2016, 20:42:59) [MSC v.1500 32 bit (
Intel)] on win32
Type "help", "copyright", "credits" or "license" for more information.
>>>
>>> 1>4
False
>>>
>>> 1>4 and 4>3
False
>>>
>>> 1>4 or 4>3
True
>>>
>>> not(4>1)
False
>>>
>>>
```

Membership operators

Python has two membership operators to test the membership in a sequence, such as a string, list, tuple, and others:

Operator	Description
in	Returns True if the specified operand is found in the sequence
not in	Returns True if the specified operand is not found in the sequence

The following screenshot will make it clearer for you:

In the preceding screenshot, we try to search for the character, `'o'`, in the string, `'John'`, and it returns `True`. However, `'k'` is not present in the string, and hence, it returns `False`.

Identity operators

Given in the table are the two identity operators:

Operator	Description
is	Returns `True` if two variables point to the same object and `False`, otherwise
is not	Returns `False` if two variables point to the same object and `True`, otherwise

The following screenshot shows that the value can be same but `id` can be different. It returns `True` if `id` is the same:

```
Python 2.7.13 Shell                                    [ _ ][ □ ][ X ]
File  Edit  Shell  Debug  Options  Window  Help
Python 2.7.13 (v2.7.13:a06454b1afa1, Dec 17 2016, 20:42:59) [MSC v.15
00 32 bit (Intel)] on win32
Type "copyright", "credits" or "license()" for more information.
>>>
>>> x=10
>>> y=10
>>> id(x)
31564396
>>> id(y)
31564396
>>> x is y
True
>>> x=[1,2,3]
>>> y=[1,2,3]
>>> x is y
False
>>> print x==y
True
>>> id(x)
43508880
>>> id(y)
43507624
>>>
>>> |




                                                        Ln: 23  Col: 4
```

Here, as both x and y contain the same value (10), id() returns the same value for both. However, when x and y are provided with the same list, id() returns different values. This could be attributed to the fact that when x and y have 10 assigned to them, it essentially means that both are pointing to the same memory address, which has a value of 10, while in the case of a list, this could be different. Why different? That is because lists are immutable, which means they can't be changed. So, when we assign the same list to y, it means that a new memory address is blocked again for a new list.

The id() function returns the *identity* of an object. This is an integer (or long integer), which is guaranteed to be unique and constant for this object during its lifetime. It is similar to memory addresses in the C language.

However, there is a small twist in our `id()` function. Python supports same memory allocation for integers only up to `256`. It will be clearer with the following screenshot:

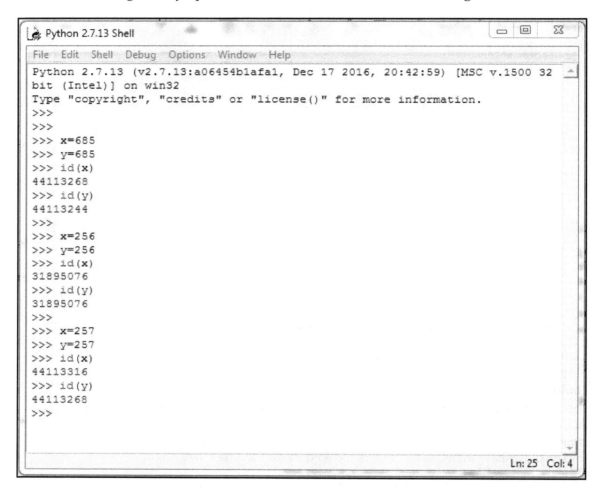

Here, as you can see, once we pass values above `256` for x and y, both are given different memory allocations by the interpreter, but if the values are `256`, then the same memory allocation is provided for both x and y.

Operator precedence

Operators with the highest precedence are placed on the top:

Operator	Description
( )	Parentheses
`x[index],x[index1:index2],f(arg...),x.attribute`	Subscription, slicing, call, and attribute reference
`**`	Exponentiation
`+x, -x, ~x`	Positive, negative, and bitwise *NOT*
`*, /, %`	Multiplication, division, and remainder
`+, -`	Addition and subtraction
`<<, >>`	Shifts
`&`	Bitwise *AND*
`^`	Bitwise *XOR*
`|`	Bitwise *OR*
`in, not in, is, is not, <, <=, >, >=, !=, ==`	Comparisons, including membership tests and identity tests
`not x`	Boolean *NOT*
`and`	Boolean *AND*
`or`	Boolean *OR*
`if...else`	Conditional expression
`lambda`	Lambda expression

Operators that have the same precedence are evaluated from left to right, except for comparisons and exponentiation. Comparisons can be chained arbitrarily.

Summary

In this chapter, you learned about various data types available in Python and the naming conventions required. You also learned about the Python character set and about converting a character set to ASCII code and vice versa, using `ord()` and `chr()` methods available in the language. In the next chapter, you will learn about two different data types, namely string and tuples.

3
Strings

In this chapter, you will learn Python strings and tuples. You will learn how to use string, string slicing, string methods, and useful functions. You will learn what is an immutable sequence. In the tuple section, you will see how to use the Python tuple.

Python strings

A Python string is a sequence, which consists of zero or more characters. The string is an immutable data structure, which means they cannot be changed. For example, if you define string str1 = "Satyamev jayate", then str1 will always remain "Satyamev jayate". You cannot edit the value of the str1 variable. Although you can reassign str1, let's discuss this with examples:

```
>>> str1 = "satyamev jayate"
>>> str1
'satyamev jayate'
>>> id(str1)
47173288
```

In the preceding example, a "satyamev jayate" string has been assigned to an str1 variable. By using the ID function, we obtained the memory address. Now, reassign the str1 variable as shown here:

```
>>> str1 = "Leapx"
>>> id(str1)
44909408
>>>
```

You can see that the memory address of the `str1` variable has been changed. But string value at memory address `47173288` will not change. Python memory management might delete the value if it is not referred by any variable. If the value exists at memory address, then you can get the value using `ctypes` modules as shown here:

```
>>> import ctypes
>>> ctypes.cast(47173288, ctypes.py_object).value
'satyamev jayate'
>>>
```

In order to find the length of the string, the `len()` function is used as shown in the following example:

```
>>> a = "hello jarvis"
>>> len(a)
12
>>> b= ""
>>> len(b)
0
>>>
```

Sometimes, you may want to access a particular character(s) at a given position in the string. The subscript operator makes this possible.

The subscript operator

The subscript operator is defined as square brackets `[]`. It is used to access the elements of string, list tuple, and so on. Let's discuss the syntax with an example:

```
<given string>[<index>]
```

The `given string` is the string you want to examine and the `index` is the position of the character you want to obtain. Let's discuss this with an example:

```
>>> name = "The Avengers"
>>> name[0]
'T'
>>> len(name)
12
>>> name[11]
's'
>>>
>>> name[12]
 Traceback (most recent call last):
  File "<pyshell#6>", line 1, in <module>
```

```
        name[12]
IndexError: string index out of range
>>>
```

The "`The Avengers`" string is 12 characters long, which means it ranges from 0 to 11 index. The `name[0]` represents the character '`T`'. If you give the 12th index value, then the Python interpreter generates an error out of range.

Let's see what is negative indexing:

```
>>> name[-1]
's'
>>> name[-12]
'T'
>>>
```

The `-1` index represents the last character and `-12` represents the first character.

In the computer world, the computer counts the index from 0 itself.

The following diagram will clear all your doubts:

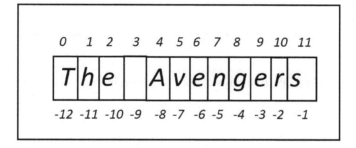

Positive and negative indexing

Slicing for substrings

In many situations, you might need a particular portion of strings such as the first three characters of the string. Python's subscript operator uses slicing. In slicing, colon : is used. An integer value will appear on either side of the colon. Refer to the following example:

```
>>>
>>> name[0:3]
'The'
>>> name[:6]
```

```
'The Av'
>>> name[4:]
'Avengers'
>>> name[5:9]
'veng'
>>>

>>> name[::2]
'TeAegr'
>>>
```

Refer to the following diagram to clear your remaining doubts:

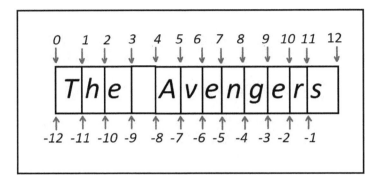

String positive and negative slicing

 If you want to print a reverse of the given string `str1`, then use `str1[::-1]`

To find the length of a string, you can use the `len()` function:

```
>>> len(name)
12
>>>
```

Now, let's see some useful string methods.

Python string methods

There are several string methods, which will be discussed one by one. To represent strings, we use the `str1` variable.

Sometimes, we want to count the characters or substrings in the given string. The string method `count` helps to achieve this:

```
count()
```

The syntax for the method is as follows:

```
str1.count(substr [, start [, end]])
```

The count method returns the number of occurrences of the substring `substr` in string `str1`. By using the parameter `start` and `end` you can obtain a slice of `str1`.

Consider the following example:

```
>>> str1 = 'The Avengers'
>>> str1.count("e")
3
>>> str1.count("e",5,12)
2
>>>
```

In many situations, we need to find the index of the substring in the given string. The `find()` method can do the task.

The syntax for the `find()` method is given as follows:

```
str.find(str, beg=0 end=len(string))
```

The `find()` method is used to find out whether a string occurs in a given string or its substrings.

```
>>> str1 = "peace begins with a smile"
>>> str1.find("with")
13
>>>
```

So 13 is the index value of substring "with" as shown here:

```
peace begins with a smile
───────────────13
```

Showing index value of substring

Let's discuss another example of the find method:

```
>>> str1 = "what we think, we become"
>>> str1.find("we")
5
>>>
```

In the preceding example, the "we" substring occurs two times, but the find method will only give the index of the first occurrence. If you want to find the occurrence from right, you can use the rfind method. Let's learn by example:

```
> str1 = "what we think, we become"
>> str1.rfind("we")
15
>>>
```

Sometimes, the user wants to find the index of a substring but is not sure about the cases. The substring may occur in lower, upper, or title cases. Python gives you some methods to deal with cases.

String case methods

Let's see one by one, first is the lower() method.

The syntax for the lower() method is given as follows:

```
str1.lower()
```

The lower() method returns a string in which all case-based characters are present in lowercase. Let's see an example:

```
>>> name = "Mohit RAJ1234"
>>> name.lower()
'mohit raj1234'
>>> name
```

```
'Mohit RAJ1234'
>>>
```

You can see that case-based characters get converted into lowercase; as we know that the string is immutable, the original string remains the same. If you like uppercase, you can use the upper () method.

The syntax for the upper () method is given as follows:

```
str1.upper()
```

The upper method returns a copy of string str1, which contains all uppercase characters. Consider the following example:

```
>>> name = "Hello jarvis"
>>> name.upper()
'HELLO JARVIS'
>>> name
'Hello jarvis'
>>>
```

Sometimes, we need to capitalize the first character of the line. In this case, the capitalize() method allows you to do that for you.

The syntax for the method is given as follows:

```
str1.capitalize()
```

This method capitalizes the first letter of the returned string:

```
>>> name = "the game"
>>> name.capitalize()
'The game'
>>>
```

If you want to convert the first character of every word of the string in uppercase, you can use the title() method:

The syntax for the method is given as follows:

```
str1.title()
```

The title() method returns a copy of the string in which the first character of every word of the string is capitalized:

```
>>> name = 'genesis of a new realm of possibility.'
>>> name.title()
'Genesis Of A New Realm Of Possibility.'
```

```
>>> name
'genesis of a new realm of possibility.'
>>>
```

A `swapcase` method allows the user to swap the cases:

```
swapcase()
```

The syntax for it is as follows:

```
str.swapcase()
```

It returns a copy of the string in which the cases are swapped.

Consider the following example:

```
>>> name = 'Genesis Of A New Realm Of Possibility.'
>>> name.swapcase()
'gENESIS oF a nEW rEALM oF pOSSIBILITY.'
>>>
>>> name
'Genesis Of A New Realm Of Possibility.'
>>>
```

String strip methods

Dealing with the strings, many times programmers encounter the problem of undesirable character/characters at the end or beginning of the string, such as space or new line character at the end, for example, `" Baba saheb "` and `"Dr Ambedkar n"`.

To handle these problems, the Python string class comes loaded with three methods. We will discuss them one by one. Let's start with `rstrip()`.

The syntax for the method is given as follows:

```
str1.rstrip([chars])
```

This method returns a copy of string `str1` in which unwanted character/characters get removed from the right side of the string.

Consider the following example:

```
>>> str1 = "Dr Ambedkarn"
>>> str1.rstrip("n")
'Dr Ambedkar'
```

If you do not provide any *chars* as argument, then space is taken as default. Look at following the example:

```
>>> str2 =  " Baba Saheb "
>>> str2.rstrip()
' Baba Saheb'
>>>
```

If you want to strip from the left-side use the `lstrip()` method. If you want to strip from both sides, use the `strip()` method.

Consider the following example:

```
>>> str2
' Baba Saheb '
>>> str2.strip()
'Baba Saheb'
>>>
```

String split methods

Sometimes we see strings in the form of parts such as `"27-12-2016"` and `"Mohit raj"`. Our requirement is to get the last part or first part. So, based upon delimiters, we can split strings into parts and take the desirable part. Let's understand how it works; from the first string, we need only the year part.

We have an interesting method called `split()`.

The syntax for the method is given as follows:

```
Str1.split("delimiter", num)
```

Let's look at an example:

```
>>> str1.split("-", 1)
['27', '12-2016']
>>>
```

The `split` method returns a list of all the words of the string separated by a delimiter and the `num` integer specifies the maximum splits. If `num` is not specified, then all the possible splits are made. Refer to the following example:

```
>>> str1 = "27-12-2016"
>>> str1.split("-")
['27', '12', '2016']
```

```
>>>
```

So far, we have not learned about lists, which we will be covering later. But using this method, we can access a particular value of the list:

```
>>> list1 = str1.split("-")
>>> list1[2]
'2016'
>>>
```

If you don't provide any delimiter, then the space is taken as the default, as shown here:

```
>>> name = "Mohit raj"
>>> name.split()
['Mohit', 'raj']
>>>
```

If you want that splits should be started from the right, then you can use the `rsplit()` method, as shown in the following example:

```
>>> str1 = "27-12-2016"
>>> str1.rsplit("-", 1)
['27-12', '2016']
>>>
```

I hope you got the idea of splitting.

String justify methods

methods to deal with these types of situations.

In many situations, you might need to justify the string length. The requirement may be string, which must possess a certain length. We have four string methods to deal with these types of situations. Let's start from ljust(), which means left justify.

The syntax for the method is given as follows:

```
str1.ljust(width[, fillchar])
```

When you provide the string to the `ljust()` method, it returns the string left justified. The minimum string length is specified by width and the padding on the left side is specified by the `fillchar` character(s), the space is default.

Consider the following examples:

```
>>> str1= "Mohit Raj"
```

```
>>> str1.ljust(15, "#")
'Mohit Raj######'
>>>
>>> str2= "Bhaskar Narayan Das"
>>> str2.ljust(15, "#")
'Bhaskar Narayan Das'
>>>
```

In the preceding example, the length of str2 is greater than 15. So padding is not made, which means fillchars has not been used. Let's see the example of rjust, which does the same thing but justifies the length from the right side:

```
>>> str1= "Mohit Raj"
>>> str1.rjust(15, "#")
'######Mohit Raj'
>>>
```

Consider the situation where you want to justify the string from both sides. In this case, we will use the center() method.

Let's see an example of center():

```
>>> str1= "Mohit Raj"
>>> str1.center(16, "#")
'###Mohit Raj####'
>>>
```

Sometimes when you are dealing with strings such as bank account number, binary numbers, and so on, you may need to justify the string with zeros. Although we can do this using the ljust method, Python offers you a special method called zfill().

The syntax for the method is given as follows:

```
str.zfill(width)
```

This method pads the string on the left with zeros to fill the width.

Consider the following examples:

```
>>> acc_no =  "3214567987"
>>> acc_no.zfill(15)
'000003214567987'
>>>
>>> binary_num = "10101010"
>>> binary_num.zfill(16)
'0000000010101010'
>>>
```

Strings

Many times we deal with the situation where we may want to replace a word from a line or a substring from the string. Python's `replace()` string method can do the task.

replace()

The syntax for the method is as follows:

```
str.replace(old, new max)
```

This method returns a copy of the string in which the old character(s) are replaced with new character(s). The `max` parameter specifies the number of replacements. If no number is specified, then it means all the occurrences would be replaced.

Consider the following example:

```
>>> str1 = "time is great and time is money"
>>> str1.replace("is","was")
'time was great and time was money'
>>>
>>> str1
'time is great and time is money'
>>> str1.replace("is",1)
>>> str1.replace("is","was",1)
'time was great and time is money'
>>>
```

Consider you have a sequence (list or tuple) of string and you want to join values of the sequence.

Consider the sequence `["Mohit","raj"]` and you want to make it `"Mohit raj"` or `"Mohit-raj"`.

To deal with these type of situations, use the `join` method:

```
join()
```

The syntax for the method is:

```
str1.join(seq)
```

The `seq` contains the sequence of separated strings; here, `str1` acts as a separator. Let's see different examples of `join()`:

1. The space as the separator:

```
>>> name = ["Mohit","raj"]
>>> " ".join(name)
```

```
'Mohit raj'
>>>
```

2. Nothing as separator:

```
>>> "".join(name)
'Mohitraj'
>>>
```

3. A hyphen – as the separator:

```
>>> "-".join(name)
'Mohit-raj'
>>>
```

You can try with different-2 separators.

String Boolean methods

Let's discuss some string methods, which return the value in the form of `True` or `False` based upon certain conditions. Sometime we are interested in strings which are ends with particular substring. For this we use string method endswith()

The syntax of the method is as follows:

```
str1.endswith(sub-string, begin,end)
```

The method returns `True` if string `str1` ends with specified substring. The `begin` and `end` parameter represent the slice of string `str1`:

Consider the following example:

```
>>> str1 = "Life should be great rather than long"
>>> str1.endswith("ng")
True
>>>
>>> str1.endswith("er")
False
>>> str1.endswith("er",0,27)
True
>>>
```

The next method is `startswith()`, which works the same way as the previous method, just check the condition from the beginning.

Let's understand with the help of an example:

```
>>> str1.startswith("Li")
True
>>> str1.startswith("be", 11)
False
>>> str1.startswith("be", 12, 16)
True
>>>
```

Consider you may want to be sure that the given string must contain only letters. The `isalpha()` methods helps you to do that.

The syntax is given as follows:

```
Str1.isalpha()
```

The method returns `True` only if string `str1` contains letters alone.

Consider the following example:

```
>>> str1 = "Hello"
>>> str1.isalpha()
True
>>> str2 = "Hello 123"
>>> str2.isalpha()
False
>>> str3 = "hello "
>>> str2.isalpha()
False
>>>
```

Even spaces are not allowed.

If you want to check the alphanumeric characters appearing in the string, then you can use the `isalnum()` method. This method returns `True` if the string contains only alphanumeric characters.

Consider the following examples:

```
>>> str1 = "Hello123"
>>> str1.isalnum()
True
>>> str2 = "Hello123#"
>>> str2.isalnum()
False
>>>
```

If you only want to check digits, then you can use the `isdigit()` method.

The syntax is given as follows:

```
str.isdigit()
```

This method returns `True` if the string contains only digits.

Consider the following example:

```
>>> str1 = "12345"
>>> str1.isdigit()
True
>>>
>>> str2 = "123456H"
>>> str2.isdigit()
False
```

To deal with only white spaces, Python string offers a method called `isspace()`, which returns `True` if the string contains only spaces:

```
isspace()
```

The syntax is given as follows:

```
str.isspace()
```

Consider the following example:

```
>>> str1 = "hello "
>>> str1.isspace()
False
>>> str2 = " "
>>> str2.isspace()
True
>>>
```

Let's see methods that deal with cases:

```
istitle()
```

The syntax is given as follows:

```
str.istitle()
```

The `istitle()` method returns `True` if the string is in title case. The following example shows the rest of the story:

```
>>> str1 = "Mohit raj"
>>> str1.istitle()
False
>>> str2 = "Mohit Raj"
>>> str2.istitle()
True
>>>
```

To check for lowercase, we can use the `islower()` method.

The syntax for the method is given as follows:

```
str.islower()
```

This method returns `True` if the string contains all lowercase characters:

```
>>> str1 = "mohit"
>>> str1.islower()
True
>>>
>>> str1 = "Mohit"
>>> str1.islower()
False
>>> str2 = "mohit1234"
>>> str2.islower()
True
>>> str3 = "!@mohit"
>>> str3.islower()
True
>>>
```

The `islower()` method does not care about the special character and digits.

Similarly, to check for uppercase you can use `isupper()`:

```
isupper()
```

The syntax is given as follows:

```
str.isupper()
```

This method returns `True` if the string contains only uppercase characters:

```
>>> str1 = "MOHIT"
>>> str1.isupper()
True
>>> str2 = "MOHIT123#$"
>>> str2.isupper()
True
>>> str3 = "mOHIT"
>>> str3.isupper()
False
>>>
```

String functions

So far you have seen string methods. Let's see built-in functions of sequences and what values they would return when the string is passed as an argument. At the beginning of the chapter, we have already discussed the `len()` function.

Consider you need to find the minimum character from a given string according to the ASCII value. To handle this situation, you can use the `min()` function:

```
min()
```

The syntax is given as follows:

```
min(str1)
```

The `min()` function returns the min character from string `str1` according to the ASCII value:

```
>>> str1 = "Life should be great rather than long"
>>> min(str1)
' '
>>> str2 = "hello!"
>>> min(str2)
'!'
>>>
```

The next method is `max()`, which returns the max characters from string `str` according to the ASCII value. Let's see some examples:

```
>>> str1 = "Life should be great rather than long"
>>> max(str1)
'u'
>>> str2 = "hello!"
>>> max(str2)
'o'
>>>
```

In many situations, we might need to convert integers or floats into a string. In order to do this conversion, the `str()` function is used.

The syntax is given as follows:

```
str(value)
```

This function converts an argument value to string type. The argument value can be any type.

Consider the following examples:

```
>>> a = 123
>>> type(a)
<type 'int'>
>>> str(a)
'123'
>>> list1 = [1,2]
>>> type(list1)
<type 'list'>
>>> str(list1)
'[1, 2]'
```

In order to find a substring in the string, you can use the `in` operator. The `in` operator is used with the if statement as shown in the following example:

```
>>> str1 = "Life should be great rather than long"
>>> if "be" in str1:
            print "yes"


yes
>>>
```

You have gained enough knowledge on Python strings. Now we move on to our next immutable data structure.

Tuple

Python tuple is a sequence, which can store heterogeneous data types such as integers, floats, strings, lists, and dictionaries. Like strings, tuple is immutable.

Creating an empty tuple

```
<variable -name > = ()
Tup1 = ()
```

The empty tuple is written as two parentheses containing nothing.

Creating tuple with elements

To create a tuple, fill the values in tuple separated by commas:

```
tup1 = (1,2,3,4.6, "hello", "a")
```

If you define the variable as follows:

```
a = 1,2,3
```

The variable a would be a tuple:

```
>>> tup1 = 1,2,3,4
>>> tup1
(1, 2, 3, 4)
>>>
>>> type(tup1)
<type 'tuple'>
>>>
```

Indexing tuple

In order to access a particular value of tuple, specify a position number, in brackets. Let's discuss with an example. I am going to make a tuple of the heroes from the movie *Avengers*.

```
>>> Avengers = ("iron-man", "vision", "Thor", "hulk")
>>> Avengers[0]
'iron-man'
>>> Avengers[2]
'Thor'
>>>
>>> Avengers[-1]
'hulk'
>>>
```

The following diagram will clear the doubts:

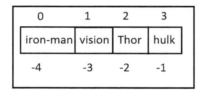

Tuple indexing

Now you can see positive and negative indexing.

Slicing of tuple

In order to do slicing, use the square brackets with the index or indices.

Consider the following example:

```
>>> Avengers[1:3]
('vision', 'Thor')
>>>
```

Let's discuss with this diagram:

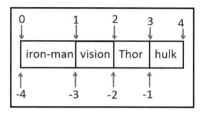

Slicing of tuple

```
>>> Avengers[:3]
('iron-man', 'vision', 'Thor')
```

The preceding example means we need start from 0 to 3:

```
>>> Avengers[1:]
('vision', 'Thor', 'hulk')
>>>
```

The preceding example means we start from 1 to the last index.

If you use slicing index out of range, then the empty tuple would be returned:

```
>>> Avengers[5:6]
()
```

For negative indexing, use the following code:

```
>>> Avengers[-3:-2]
('vision',)
>>>
```

Now, let's see some generic function, which can be applied on the tuple.

Unpacking the items of tuples

In this section, we will learn how to unpack the tuple variable. Let's learn by example:

```
>>> tup1 = (1,2,3)
>>> a,b,c = tup1
>>> a
1
>>> b
2
>>> c
3
```

In the preceding example, tuple's items have been assigned to a, b, and c variables correspondingly.

What happens if you use more number of variables than the number of items in a tuple. Let's see more examples:

```
>>> tup2 = (5,6)
>>> x,y,z = tup2

Traceback (most recent call last):
 File "<pyshell#11>", line 1, in <module>
 x,y,z = tup2
ValueError: need more than 2 values to unpack
```

So, interpreter throws a ValueError.

What happens if you use less number of variables than the number of items in a tuple. Let's see more examples:

```
>>> tup2 = (5,6)
>>> x,y,z = tup2

Traceback (most recent call last):
 File "<pyshell#11>", line 1, in <module>
 x,y,z = tup2
ValueError: need more than 2 values to unpack
```

So, the interpreter once again shows an error with a different description.

Tuple functions

If you want to know the length of the tuple, then you can use the `len()` function.

len()

The syntax for the method is as follows:

```
len(tuple)
```

The `len()` function returns the length of the tuple, which means the total number of elements in a tuple.

```
>>> tup1 = ("C", "Python", "java","html")
>>> len(tup1)
4
>>>
```

Let's see how to use the `max()` function on a tuple.

max()

The syntax for the method is as follows:

```
max(tuple)
```

The `max(tuple)` function returns the element of tuple with the maximum value.

You must be in doubt with the meaning of maximum value.

Let's understand with examples:

```
>>> t2 = (1,2,3,4,510)
>>> max(t2)
510
```

The `max` function returns the maximum integer value.

If the tuple contains int and float with the same numeric value, which value would be returned can you guess? Let's see with this example:

```
>>> t2 = (1,2,450.0,450)
>>> max(t2)
450.0
>>>
```

If you are thinking it returns a float value, see the next example:

```
>>> t2 = (1,2,450,450.0)
>>> max(t2)
450
>>>
```

Both `450` and `450.0` possess the same numeric value. The `max` function returns the first occurrence in the tuple:

```
>>> t3 = (800, "1")
>>> max(t3)
'1'
>>>
```

The `max()` function returns the string as the max value.

Let's see an example of string comparison:

```
>>> tup1 = ('aa', 'z', "az")
>>> max(tup1)
'z'
>>>
```

The max value decision is taken on the basis of the first character. So, `'z'` has been taken as the max value.

Let's see the next example:

```
>>> tup2 = ('aa', 'z', "az", "za")
>>> max(tup2)
'za'
>>>
```

You can see that the second and fourth strings both have the `'z'` character in the first position; this is when the decision is taken by judging the second character.

min()

The syntax for this method is as follows:

```
min(tuple)
```

The `min(tuple)` function returns the element of tuple with a minimum value.

Consider the following examples:

```
>>> tup1 = (1,2,3,4,"1")
>>> min(tup1)
1
>>> tup2 = ('aa', 'z', "az")
>>> min(tup2)
'aa'
>>>
```

If you want to convert a string or list into a tuple, then you can use the `tuple()` function.

Consider the following example:

```
>>> str1 = "mohit"
>>> tuple(str1)
('m', 'o', 'h', 'i', 't')
>>>
```

You can delete the tuple using `del` keyword, as shown in the following example:

```
>>> tup1 = (1,2,3)
>>> tup1
(1, 2, 3)
>>> del tup1
>>> tup1

Traceback (most recent call last):
  File "<pyshell#25>", line 1, in <module>
  tup1
NameError: name 'tup1' is not defined
>>>
```

Operations of tuples

In this section, you will see addition and multiplication.

By using the + operator, two tuples can be added as shown:

```
>>> avenger1 = ("Iron-man", "captain", "Thor")
>>> avenger2 = ("Vision", "Sam")
>>> avenger1 + avenger2
('Iron-man', 'captain', 'Thor', 'Vision', 'Sam')
>>>
```

By using the * operator, you can perform multiplication:

```
>>> language = ("Python","html")
>>> language*2
('Python', 'html', 'Python', 'html')
>>>
```

Let's check the memory address of the tuple after multiplication:

```
>>> a = language*2
>>> a
('Python', 'html', 'Python', 'html')
>>> id(a[0])
45826944
>>>
>>> id(a[2])
45826944
>>>
>>> id(a[1])
45828896
>>> id(a[3])
45828896
>>>
```

Now, you can see that the first and third strings both possess the same memory location.

Exercise

1. Obtain the domain (thapar.edu) name from the URL
   `http://www.thapar.edu/index.php/about-us/mission`.

2. You have the tuple `tup = ('www', 'thapar', 'edu','index',
   'php','about-us','mission');` now you can make a full URL like this
   `www.thapar.edu/index.php/about-us/mission`

Summary

In this chapter, you have learned about strings, how to define strings, string functions, and string methods. Strings are immutable, they cannot be changed. In the tuple section, you have seen how to create a tuple. Like strings, tuples are immutable. There is no method that exists, which can change the existing tuple or string.

4
Lists

In this chapter, we will cover Python lists, list functions, and list methods.

In the real world, we often make lists, such as daily to-do lists, a list of players of the Cricket team, a guest list for a wedding, lists of food, and so on.

Like tuple, a list is also a built-in data structure available in Python. It can contain heterogeneous values such as integers, floats, strings, tuples, lists, and dictionaries. However, Python lists are mutable; yes, they can change.

The following are the characteristics of a Python list:

- Values are ordered
- Mutable
- A list can hold any number of values
- A list can add, remove, and alter the values

Creating a list

Let's see how we can create an empty list:

```
<Variable name > = []
List1 = []
```

Creating a list with values

A list contains comma-separated values. For example:

```
Avengers = ['hulk', 'iron-man', 'Captain', 'Thor']
```

Unpacking list values

You can assign a list value to variables by using the assignment operator. Let's discuss this with an example:

```
>>> a,b = [1,2]

>>> a

1

>>> b

2

>>>
```

You can see that 1 is assigned to variable a and 2 is assigned to variable b. This is called **unpacking**. What happens when a list is provided with more variables? Let's see the following example:

```
>>> a,b = [1,2,3]
Traceback (most recent call last):

  File "<pyshell#7>", line 1, in <module>

    a,b = [1,2,3]

ValueError: too many values to unpack
```

The error indicates that there are more values to unpack. Let's see another example:

```
>>> a,b,c = [1,2]
Traceback (most recent call last):

  File "<pyshell#8>", line 1, in <module>

    a,b,c = [1,2]

ValueError: need more than 2 values to unpack
```

The preceding error indicates that there should be more list values to unpack.

List operations

In this section, you will learn slicing, accessing, adding, deleting, and updating the values in a list.

Accessing list values

In order to access list values, use list names with positional index in square brackets. For example, consider the following code snippet:

```
>>> Avengers = ['hulk', 'iron-man', 'Captain', 'Thor']

>>> Avengers[0]

'hulk'

>>> Avengers[3]

'Thor'

>>> Avengers[-1]

'Thor'

>>> Avengers[4]

Traceback (most recent call last):

  File "<pyshell#5>", line 1, in <module>

    Avengers[4]

IndexError: list index out of range
```

If the desired index is not found in the list, then the interpreter throws IndexError.

Slicing the list

The slicing of a list is the same as we did in tuples. See the syntax:

```
<list-name>[start : stop : step]
```

See the example:

```
>>> Avengers[1:3]

['iron-man', 'Captain']

>>> Avengers[:4]

['hulk', 'iron-man', 'Captain', 'Thor']

>>> Avengers[:]

['hulk', 'iron-man', 'Captain', 'Thor']

>>> Avengers[2:]

['Captain', 'Thor']

>>> list1 = [1,2,3,4,5,6,7,8,9,10,11,12,13]

>>> list1[1:13:3]

[2, 5, 8, 11]

>>>
```

The step means the amount by which the index increases. If you don't define it, then it takes 1 step by default.

Updating the list

Lists are mutable, so the values of a list can be updated.

Let's see the example with our mightiest heroes of Avengers:

```
Avengers = ['hulk', 'iron-man', 'Captain', 'Thor']
```

In the preceding list, the name 'Captain' should be 'Captain-America':

```
>>> Avengers = ['hulk', 'iron-man', 'Captain', 'Thor']

>>> Avengers[2]

'Captain'

>>> Avengers[2] = "Captain-America"
```

```
>>> Avengers

['hulk', 'iron-man', 'Captain-America', 'Thor']

>>>
```

By using the index number, you can update the values.

Deleting values from a list

By using the `del` keyword, you can delete a value or a slice of list from the list.

Let's see the example of making a new team for the *Civil* War movie:

```
>>> C_W_team = ['hulk', 'iron-man', 'Captain-America', 'Thor',"Vision"]

>>> del C_W_team[0]

>>> C_W_team

['iron-man', 'Captain-America', 'Thor', 'Vision']

>>>

>>> del C_W_team[2:4]

>>> C_W_team

['iron-man', 'Captain-America']

>>>
```

We deleted the first and last two values from the list in the preceding example.

Addition of Python lists

You can add two lists by using the + operator.

See the following example:

```
>>> Avengers1 = ['hulk', 'iron-man', 'Captain-America', 'Thor']

>>> Avengers2 = ["Vision","sam"]

>>>
```

We need a big team, so add both the lists:

```
>>> Avengers1+Avengers2

['hulk', 'iron-man', 'Captain-America', 'Thor', 'Vision', 'sam']

>>>

>>> Avengers2+Avengers1

['Vision', 'sam', 'hulk', 'iron-man', 'Captain-America', 'Thor']

>>>

>>> Avengers1

['hulk', 'iron-man', 'Captain-America', 'Thor']

>>>

>>> Avengers2

['Vision', 'sam']

>>>
```

The original list will not be changed; the addition of lists can be saved to another variable.

Multiplication of lists

By using the * operator, you can perform multiplication of Python lists, as shown in the following example:

```
>>> Av = ['Vision', 'sam']

>>> new_Av = Av*2

>>> new_Av

['Vision', 'sam', 'Vision', 'sam']

Let us see the memory address of the  new list.

>>> id(new_Av[0])

47729312
```

```
>>> id(new_Av[2])

47729312

>>>
```

In this case, the memory address of both the index values is the same.

in operator

You can use the in operator on list with the if statement.

Let's discuss this with an example:

```
>>> Avengers= ['hulk', 'iron-man', 'Captain-America', 'Thor']
>>> if "iron-man" in Avengers:

                  print "yes "



yes

>>>

>>> if "vision" in Avengers:

                  print "yes "



>>>
```

In the preceding example, we check whether the particular value exists in the list or not. We check whether the strings, "iron-man" and "vision", exist in the Avengers list.

This way, you can use the in operator in a list.

List functions

In this section, we will discuss some Python built-in functions, which can be applied to a list.

len()

The syntax for the len() method is given as follows:

```
len(list)
```

The `len()` function returns the number of elements or values in the list, as shown in the following example:

```
>>> avengers = ['hulk', 'iron-man', 'Captain-America', 'Thor']

>>> len(avengers)

4

>>>
```

Let'ss see how to use the `max ()` function on a list.

max ()

The syntax for the `max ()` method is given as follows:

```
max (list)
```

The `max (list)` function returns the element of the list with the maximum value:

```
>>> list1 = [1, 2, 3, 4,510]

>>> max (list1)

510

>>> list1 = [1, 2, 3, 4,510,510.0]

>>> max (list1)

510
```

```
>>> list1 = [1, 2, 3, 4,510.0, 510]

>>> max (list1)

510.0

>>> list2 = [800, "1"]

>>> max (list2)

'1'

>>>
```

The working of the max () function for lists and tuples is the same. Max preference of a string is more than float and integer values.

The next function is the min () function, the opposite of the max () function. The min () function returns an element from the Python list with the minimum value.

You can easily convert a tuple into a list by using the list () function.

list ()

The syntax for the list () method is given as follows:

```
list(tuple)
```

The list function converts the sequence into a list. Let's see the following example:

```
>>> tup1 = ("a","b","c")

>>> list (tup1)

['a', 'b', 'c']

>>> name = "mohit raj"

>>> list1(name)

>>> list (name)

['m', 'o', 'h', 'i', 't', ' ', 'r', 'a', 'j']

>>>
```

You can see that the tuple, `tup1`, and string name have been converted into a list.

Python offers you a function to sort the list, called `sorted ()`.

sorted ()

The syntax for the `sorted ()` method is given as follows:

```
sorted (iterable, cmp, key, reverse)
```

The `sorted ()` function returns a new sorted list from the values in *iterable*. See the following example:

```
>>> list1 = [2, 3, 0, 3, 1, 4, 7, 1]

>>> sorted (list1)

[0, 1, 1, 2, 3, 3, 4, 7]

>>> list1

[2, 3, 0, 3, 1, 4, 7, 1]

>>>
```

Let's take a tuple to pass into the `sorted()` function, as shown in the following:

```
>>> tup1 = (2, 3, 0, 3, 1, 4, 7, 1)

>>> sorted (tup1)

[0, 1, 1, 2, 3, 3, 4, 7]

>>> tup1

[2, 3, 0, 3, 1, 4, 7, 1]

>>>
```

In the preceding example, you saw that the return type is `list`. So, the `sorted ()` function always returns a `list` type. We will see the rest of the arguments of the `sorted ()` function in the list method, `sort ()`.

List methods

In this section, we will discuss list methods, one by one, with examples.

Let's make an empty list and add values one by one:

```
Avengers = []
```

In order to add a value to the list, we will use the `append ()` method. You will see this method most of the time.

append ()

The syntax for the `append ()` method is given as follows:

```
list.append ()
```

The method adds a value at the end of the list. Let's see the following example:

```
>>> Avengers = []

>>> Avengers.append("Captain-America")

>>> Avengers.append("Iron-man")

>>> Avengers

['Captain-America', 'Iron-man']

>>>
```

You can see that we have added two members to the list.

Consider a situation where you want to add a list to an existing list. For example, we have two lists of our heroes:

```
Avengers1 = ['hulk', 'iron-man', 'Captain-America', 'Thor']

Avengers2 = ["Vision","sam"]
```

We want to add the `Avengers2` list to the `Avengers1` list. If you are thinking about the + operator, you might be right to some extent but not completely because the + operator just shows the addition but doesn't change the original lists.

In order to add one list to another, we will use the `extend ()` method. See the syntax explained in the subsequent subsection.

extend ()

The syntax for the `extend ()` method is given as follows:

```
list1.extend (seq)
```

The `list1` list is the primary list to be extended.

The `seq` argument could be a sequence, string, tuple, or list, which would be added to `list1`. The following is the example of the famous Avenger team:

```
>>> Avengers1 = ['hulk', 'iron-man', 'Captain-America', 'Thor']

>>> Avengers2 = ["Vision","sam"]

>>> Avengers1.extend(Avengers2)

>>> Avengers1

['hulk', 'iron-man', 'Captain-America', 'Thor', 'Vision', 'sam']

>>>

>>> Avengers2

['Vision', 'sam']
```

In the preceding example, you can see that the `Avenger1` team has been extended by appending all the elements of the `Avengers2` list.

Let's see one more example:

```
>>> list1 = ["mohit", "Bhaskar"]

>>> name = "leapx"

>>> list1.extend(name)

>>> list1

['mohit', 'Bhaskar', 'l', 'e', 'a', 'p', 'x']
```

```
>>>
```

In the preceding example, `list1` has been extended by appending all the characters of the string name. Let's see another example:

```
>>> Avengers1 = ['hulk', 'iron-man', 'Captain-America', 'Thor']

>>> team2 = ("vision", "Clint")

>>> Avengers1.extend(team2)

>>> Avengers1

['hulk', 'iron-man', 'Captain-America', 'Thor', 'vision', 'Clint']

>>>
```

In the preceding example, we added the `team2` tuple to the `Avengers1` list.

Difference between append and extend.

If you are confused between the `append` and `extend` methods, the following example will clear your doubts:

```
>>> Linux   = ["kali", "Ubuntu", "debian"]

>>> Linux2 = ["RHEL", "Centos"]

>>> Linux.extend(Linux2)

>>> Linux

['kali', 'Ubuntu', 'debian', 'RHEL', 'Centos']

>>>

>>>

>>> Linux   = ["kali", "Ubuntu", "debian"]

>>> Linux2 = ["RHEL", "Centos"]

>>> Linux.append(Linux2)

>>> Linux
```

```
['kali', 'Ubuntu', 'debian', ['RHEL', 'Centos']]

>>>
```

The append method gives a list within the list. The list Linux2 = ["RHEL", "Centos"] has been taken as one list. Let's proceed to the next method.

count ()

The syntax for the count () method is given as follows:

```
list1.count (item)
```

The count () method is used to find the occurrence of an item in a list. See the following example:

```
>>> list1 = ["a","c","b","c","a","h","l", 1, 2, 3, 4]

>>> list1.count ("a")

2

>>> list1.count ("c")

2

>>>

>>> list1.count ("k")

0
```

The preceding example shows that the characters, "a" and "c", occur two times. If no occurrence is found, then the method returns 0.

Consider that you have a big list and you want to find out the index of a particular item. To accomplish this, you can use the index () method.

index ()

The syntax for the index () method is given as follows:

```
list.index(item)
```

The index () method is used to find the index of a particular item in a list. For example, consider the following code snippet:

```
>>> OS = ['kali', 'Ubuntu', 'debian', 'RHEL', 'Centos']

>>> OS.index("debian")

2

>>> OS.index("mint")


Traceback (most recent call last):

  File "<pyshell#55>", line 1, in <module>

    OS.index("mint")

ValueError: 'mint' is not in list

>>>
```

From the preceding example, you can easily understand that if a list does not contain the item, then the index () method shows ValueError.

Let's see another example:

```
>>> OS = ['kali', 'Ubuntu', 'debian', 'RHEL', 'Centos','RHEL']

>>> OS.index("RHEL")

3

>>>
```

If an item occurs two times, then the index method returns the index of the first occurrence.

Consider a list of avengers ['iron-man', 'hulk', 'Thor']. As we know, one name is missing: 'Captain-America', and I want to insert 'Captain-America' in the first index. To do this, we can use the insert () method.

insert()

The syntax for the insert () method is given as follows:

```
list1.insert (index1, item)
```

index1 is the index where the item needs to be inserted. The item is the value to be inserted into list1:

```
>>> A = ['iron-man', 'hulk', 'Thor']

>>> A.insert (0,"Captain-America")

>>> A

['Captain-America', 'iron-man', 'hulk', 'Thor']

>>>
```

remove()

Sometimes, we need to remove an item from a list. So, this can be accomplished by using the remove () method. The syntax for the method is given as follows:

```
list.remove(item)
```

The remove () method is used to remove an item from a list. For example, consider the following example:

```
>>> Avengers1 = ["Iron-man","Thor","Loki","hulk"]

>>> Avengers1.remove ("Loki")

>>> Avengers1

['Iron-man', 'Thor', 'hulk']

>>>

>>>
```

Because "Loki" was not a member of the Avengers team, we removed it.

Let's consider another example:

```
>>> num = [1,2,3,4,5,6,4,1,7]

>>> num.remove(1)

>>> num
```

```
[2, 3, 4, 5, 6, 4, 1, 7]

>>>
```

In the preceding example, you can see that the remove () method just removed the first occurrence.

pop()

If you want to see a removed item, you can use the pop () method. The syntax for the method is given as follows:

```
list.pop()
```

The pop () method removes and returns the last item from the list.

Let's take the example of the famous TV series, GoT:

```
>>> GoT = ["Tyrion","Sansa", "Arya","Joffrey","Ned-Stark"]

>>> GoT.pop()

'Ned-Stark'

>>> GoT.pop()

'Joffrey'

>>> GoT

['Tyrion', 'Sansa', 'Arya']

>>>
```

In the preceding example, you can see that the pop () method returns the removed item. You can also remove any item based on the index. See the following example:

```
>>> GoT = ["Tyrion","Sansa", "Arya","Catelyn","Joffrey","Ned-Stark"]

>>> GoT = ["Tyrion","Sansa", "Arya","Catelyn","Joffrey","Ned-Stark"]

>>> GoT.pop(3)

'Catelyn'

>>> GoT
```

```
['Tyrion', 'Sansa', 'Arya', 'Joffrey', 'Ned-Stark']

>>>
```

In preceding example, index number 3, that is, `"Catelyn"` has been removed. Sometimes, you need to sort the values of a list. Python lists offer a very beautiful method called `sort ()`.

The syntax for the method is given as follows:

```
list.sort(cmp=None, key=None, reverse=False)
```

The `sort ()` method is stable and inplace. Stable means that the order of items that compare equal will be preserved. Inplace in sort does not use extra memory. Let's understand the `sort ()` method by examples.

Consider the following example where simple numbers are sorted in an ascending order:

```
>>> list1 = [5, 6, 7, 1, 4, 2, 0, 4, 2, 8]

>>> list1.sort()

>>> list1

[0, 1, 2, 2, 4, 4, 5, 6, 7, 8]

>>>
```

Let's see how to sort the list in the descending order:

```
>>> list1 = [5, 6, 7, 1, 4, 2, 0, 4, 2, 8]

>>> list1.sort (reverse=True)

>>> list1

[8, 7, 6, 5, 4, 4, 2, 2, 1, 0]

>>>
```

Now, you got an idea of the `reverse` argument. Let's take an example of a list of numbers and strings:

```
>>> list2 = [8, 7,4,2,1, "1", "a","@#", "nm"]

>>> list2.sort ()

>>> list2
```

```
[1, 2, 4, 7, 8, '1', '@#', 'a', 'nm']
```

For ascending order, the interpreter first takes the number and then strings.

For descending order, the interpreter first takes string, then numbers:

```
>>>
>>> list2 = [8, 7,4,2,1, "1", "a","@#", "nm"]
>>> list2.sort (reverse=True)
>>> list2
['nm', 'a', '@#', '1', 8, 7, 4, 2, 1]
>>>
```

Let's take some complex examples:

Consider that you have a list of tuples as follows:

```
[("a",4),("b",1),("v",5),("f",2)]
```

The tuples in the list contain two values, and you want to sort the list according to the second value of tuples.

See the following code:

```
def fun1(x):

                return x[1]

list_tup = [("a",4),("b",1),("v",5),("f",2)]

list_tup.sort(key= fun1)

print list_tup
```

In the preceding code, we defined a fun1() function, which is used as a key of the sort method. The list_tup list passes its elements one by one to the fun1(x) function, and fun1(x) returns the tuple's second element because sort would be performed according to the tuple's second element.

Output of sort of list.

I have one more example for you. Consider that you want to sort the elements of a list but based on some conditions. Consider that you have a list as follows:

```
list1 = [10,9,3,7,2,1,23,1,561,1,1,96,1]
```

You want to sort all the elements, but you want that all 1 elements must remain on the right side. It can be accomplished by the cmp argument of the sort () method.

Let's discuss a simple example:

```
list1 = [10,9,3,7,2,1,23,1,561,1,1,96,1]

def cmp1(x,y):

        return

list1.sort(cmp = cmp1)
```

In the preceding example, we have a list of unsorted numbers. We are using the cmp argument. The cmp1 function takes two arguments. These arguments come from a given list, for example, (10, 9), (9, 3), (3,7), and so on. If cmp1 returns a negative number, then ascending order sort happens, and if it returns a positive number, then descending sort happens.

In our problem, we want ascending order sort, but we also want to push all the *1s* to the right:

```
list1 = [10,9,3,7,2,1,23,1,561,1,1,96,1]

def cmp1(x,y):

        if x == 1 or y==1:
```

```
                               c = y-x
            else:
                               c = x-y
            return c


    list1.sort(cmp = cmp1)

    print list1
```

Here is the output of the program:

Showing output of list cmp argument

reverse()

Our last list method is `reverse()`. The syntax for the method is given as follows:

```
    List1.reverse()
```

The `reverse()` method reverses the items of a list. Consider the following example:

```
    >>> av = ['hulk', 'iron-man', 'Captain-America', 'Thor', 'vision', 'Clint']

    >>> av.reverse()

    >>> av

    ['Clint', 'vision', 'Thor', 'Captain-America', 'iron-man', 'hulk']

    >>>
```

List comprehensions

List comprehension is a concise way of creating lists. In this section, we will use a list with the for loop. If you have not read about the for loop so far, you can skip this section and get back after learning about the for loop, covered in Chapter 6, *Control Statements and Loops*.

Let's take a list1 list as shown:

```
list1 = [2,3,4,5,6]
```

Now, our aim is to make a new list that contains the square of the elements of list1:

```
list1 = [2,3,4,5,6]

list2 = []

for each in list1:

        list2.append(each*each)

print list2
```

The output of the program is as follows:

Square of list

The preceding code took four lines to create the desired list. By using list comprehensions, we can do the preceding stuff in just one line:

```
>>> list1 = [2, 3, 4, 5, 6]

>>> [each*each for each in list1]

[4, 9, 16, 25, 36]

>>>
```

Let's have a look at some more examples with the `if` statement.

Create a new list that would contain the square of the even numbers of a given list:

```
list1 = [2,3,4,5,6]

list2 = []

for each in list1:

        if each%2== 0:

                list2.append(each*each)

print list2
```

The output of the preceding code snippet is as follows:

```
F:\project_7days\chapter 3\program>python listsquar.py
[4, 16, 36]
F:\project_7days\chapter 3\program>
```

List with if statement

Let's do it by using list comprehension:

```
>>> list1 = [2,3,4,5,6]

>>> [each*each for each in list1 if each%2 == 0]

[4, 16, 36]

>>>
```

Exercises

1. See the following list:

   ```
   list1 = ["abc",[2,3,("mohit","the avengers")],1,2,3]
   ```

   Get the string `"avengers"`.

2. With the `for` loop, take the following list and sort it based on the sum of the values of the tuples of the list:

   ```
   [(1,5),(9,0),(12,3),(5,4),(13,6),(1,1)]
   ```

3. Use the list, `[1,2,4,5,1,1,4,1,56]`, and find the index of all the `1` elements.
4. Do the preceding exercise by using list comprehension.

Summary

In this chapter, you learned about lists, defining a list, and using a list. You also learned various list operations, such as accessing and slicing of lists. In the list functions, you learned some generic functions that can be applied to lists. You also learned list methods specific to the list. By using list methods, you learned about `sort`, `reverse`, `pop`, `append`, and `extend` methods. Finally, you learned how to use a list with the `for` loop and how to write one-line code.

5
Dictionary

So far, you have learned about strings, tuples, and lists. In this chapter, we have another useful built-in data type in Python is called **dictionary**. In a list, values are indexed by the range of numbers, but in a dictionary, values are indexed by keys.

Overview of dictionary

In Python, a dictionary is a sequence of key-value, or item, pairs separated by commas.

Consider the following example:

```
port = {22: "SSH", 23: "Telnet" , 53: "DNS", 80: "HTTP" }
```

The `port` variable refers to a dictionary that contains port numbers as keys and its protocol names as values.

Consider the following example:

```
companies = {"IBM": "International Business Machines", "L&T" :"Larsen &
Toubro"}
```

The syntax of a dictionary is as follows:

```
Dictionary_name = {key: value}
```

The key-value pair is called an **item**. The key and value are separated by a colon (:), and each item is separated by a comma (,). The items are enclosed by curly braces ({ }). An empty dictionary can be created just by using curly braces ({ }). Key features of the dictionary are:

- The key of the dictionary can not be changed
- A string, int, or float can be used as a key
- A tuple that does not contain any list can be used as a key
- Keys are unique
- Values can be anything, for example, list, string, int, and so on
- Values can be repeated
- Values can be changed
- A dictionary is an unordered collection, which means that the order in which you have entered the items in a dictionary may not be retained and you may get the items in a different order

Operations on the dictionary

As you know, a dictionary is mutable; you can add new values, and delete and update old values. In this section, you will learn accessing, deletion, updation, and addition operations.

Accessing the values of dictionary

In order to access the dictionary's values you will need the key. Consider a dictionary of networking ports: In order to access the dictionary's values you will need the key. Consider a dictionary of networking ports:

```
Port = {80: "HTTP", 23 : "Telnet", 443 : "HTTPS"}
```

Let's learn by example:

```
>>> port = {80: "HTTP", 23 : "Telnet", 443 : "HTTPS"}
>>> port[80]
'HTTP'
>>> port[443]
'HTTPS'
```

In order to access the dictionary's value, use the square brackets along with the key. What happens if the key is not in the dictionary?

```
>>> port[21]

Traceback (most recent call last):
  File "<pyshell#4>", line 1, in <module>
  port[21]
KeyError: 21
>>>
```

If the key is not found, then the interpreter shows the preceding error.

Deleting an item from the dictionary

By using the `del` keyword, you can delete the entire dictionary or the dictionary's items. If you want to delete the dictionary's items, use the following syntax:

```
del dict[key]
```

Considering the following code snippet for example:

```
>>> port = {80: "HTTP", 23 : "Telnet", 443 : "HTTPS"}
>>> del port[23]
>>> port
{80: 'HTTP', 443: 'HTTPS'}
>>>
```

If you want to delete the entire dictionary, then use the following syntax:

```
The del dict
```

Consider the following example:

```
>>> port = {80: "HTTP", 23 : "Telnet", 443 : "HTTPS"}
>>> del port
>>> port

Traceback (most recent call last):
  File "<pyshell#12>", line 1, in <module>
  port
NameError: name 'port' is not defined
>>>
```

The preceding error shows that the `port` dictionary has been deleted.

Updating the values of the dictionary

Updating the dictionary is pretty simple; just specify the key in the square bracket along with the dictionary name. The syntax is as follows:

```
dict[key] = new_value
```

Consider the following example:

```
port = {80: "HTTP", 23 : "SMTP", 443 : "HTTPS"}
```

In the preceding dictionary, the value of port 23 is "SMTP", but in reality, port number 23 is for telnet protocol. Let's update the preceding dictionary with the following code:

```
>>> port = {80: "HTTP", 23 : "SMTP", 443 : "HTTPS"}
>>> port
{80: 'HTTP', 443: 'HTTPS', 23: 'SMTP'}
>>> port[23] = "Telnet"
>>> port
{80: 'HTTP', 443: 'HTTPS', 23: 'Telnet'}
>>>
```

Adding an item to the dictionary

Adding an item to the dictionary is very simple; just specify a new key in the square brackets along with the dictionary. The syntax is as follows:

```
dict[new_key] = value
```

Consider the following example:

```
>>> port = {80: "HTTP", 23 : "Telnet"}
>>> port[110]="POP"
>>> port
{80: 'HTTP', 110: 'POP', 23: 'Telnet'}
>>>
```

In the preceding example, we added the "POP" protocol.

Dictionary functions

In this section, we will explore the built-in functions available in Python, which can be applied to dictionary. You may have seen most of the functions in the previous chapters of list and tuple. In this section, you will see how to apply those functions to a dictionary.

len()

In order to find the number of items that are present in a dictionary, you can use the `len()` function. See the following example:

```
>>> port = {80: "http", 443: "https", 23:"telnet"}
>>> len(port)
3
>>>
```

str()

Consider a situation where you want to convert a dictionary into a string; here you can use the `str()` function. The syntax of the method is as follows:

```
str(dict)
```

Consider the following example:

```
>>> port = {80: "http", 443: "https", 23:"telnet"}
>>> port
{80: 'http', 443: 'https', 23: 'telnet'}
>>> str(port)
"{80: 'http', 443: 'https', 23: 'telnet'}"
>>>
```

You can easily see the double quotes around the dictionary. Let's get the `max` key from the dictionary, using the `max()` function.

max()

If you pass a dictionary to the `max()` function, then it returns the key with the maximum worth. The syntax of the method is as follows:

```
max(dict)
```

See the following example:

```
>>> dict1 = {1:"abc",5:"hj", 43:"Dhoni", ("a","b"):"game", "hj":56}
>>> max(dict1)
('a', 'b')
```

So, the `max` function gives the tuple the maximum worth. Similarly, to get the minimum key, you can use the `min()` function.

min()

The `min()` function is just opposite to the `max()` function. It returns the dictionary's key with the lowest worth. The syntax of the method is as follows:

```
min(dict)
```

Consider the following example:

```
>>> dict1 = {1:"abc",5:"hj", 43:"Dhoni", ("a","b"):"game", "hj":56,
(1,3):"kl"}
>>> dict1
{1: 'abc', (1, 3): 'kl', 5: 'hj', 43: 'Dhoni', 'hj': 56, ('a', 'b'):
'game'}
>>> min(dict1)
1
>>>
```

Let's convert the list or tuple into a dictionary. In order to convert the list or tuple into a dictionary, the format should be as follows:

```
port = [[80,"http"],[20,"ftp"],[23,"telnet"],[443,"https"],[53,"DNS"]]
```

Alternatively, it can be as follows:

```
port = [(80,"http"),(20,"ftp"),(23,"telnet"),(443,"https"),(53,"DNS")]
```

We need pairs of two values. By using the `dict` function, we can convert the preceding list into a dictionary.

dict()

You can pass a tuple or list to the `dict()` function, but that tuple or list contain elements as pairs of two values, as shown in the next example.

The syntax of the method is as follows:

```
dict(list or tuple)
```

Let's see the conversion by example:

```
>>> port = [[80,"http"],[20,"ftp"],[23,"telnet"],[443,"https"],[53,"DNS"]]
>>> port
[[80, 'http'], [20, 'ftp'], [23, 'telnet'], [443, 'https'], [53, 'DNS']]
>>> dict(port)
{80: 'http', 443: 'https', 20: 'ftp', 53: 'DNS', 23: 'telnet'}
>>>
>>> port = [(80,"http"),(20,"ftp"),(23,"telnet"),(443,"https"),(53,"DNS")]
>>> dict(port)
{80: 'http', 443: 'https', 20: 'ftp', 53: 'DNS', 23: 'telnet'}
>>>
```

In operator on Python dictionary The in operator can be used to find the existence of a key in the dictionary. Consider the example program `inkey.py`:

```
port1 = {21: "FTP", 22:"SSH", 23: "telnet", 80: "http"}
key = int(raw_input("Enter the key "))
if key in port1:
 print "YES"
else :
 print "NO"
```

See the following screenshot for the output:

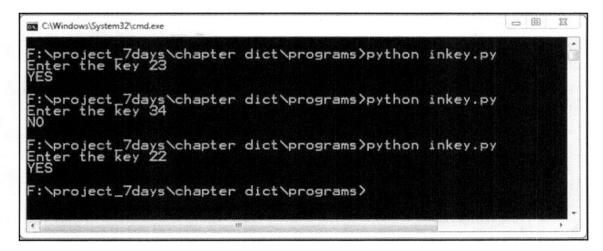

Output of in program

Similarly, you can use the `not in` operator. Consider the following example:

```
>>> port1 = {21: "FTP", 22 :"SSH", 23: "telnet", 80: "http"}
>>> if 21 not in port1:
            print "yes"
>>
```

In the preceding code snippet, nothing gets printed.

Dictionary methods

In this section, we will discuss the dictionary methods one by one. Consider that you want to create a copy of an existing dictionary; you can use the `copy()` method.

copy()

The syntax of the `copy()` method is as follows:

```
dict.copy()
```

See the following example:

```
>>> Avengers ={'iron-man':"Tony", "CA":"Steve","BW":"Natasha"}
>>> Avengers
{'iron-man': 'Tony', 'CA': 'Steve', 'BW': 'Natasha'}
>>> Avengers2 = Avengers.copy()
>>> Avengers2
{'iron-man': 'Tony', 'CA': 'Steve', 'BW': 'Natasha'}
>>>
```

You can see that `Avengers2` is an exact copy of `Avengers`. Do not confuse `copy()` with the assignment operator. Let's see the following example:

```
>>> A1 = {'iron-man':"Tony", "CA":"Steve","BW":"Natasha"}
>>> A2= A1
>>>
>>> A2
{'iron-man': 'Tony', 'CA': 'Steve', 'BW': 'Natasha'}
>>>
>>> CW= A1.copy()
>>> CW
{'iron-man': 'Tony', 'CA': 'Steve', 'BW': 'Natasha'}
>>>
```

Variable A1 and A2 hold the same dictionary, but the CW variable hold different dictionary. You can check the memory address of A1, A2, and CW:

```
>>> id(A1)
46395728
>>> id(A2)
46395728
>>> id(CW)
46136896
>>>
```

We can do one more thing. Let's add one more member to the A1 dictionary:

```
>>> A1
{'iron-man': 'Tony', 'CA': 'Steve', 'BW': 'Natasha'}
>>> A1["hulk"]= "Bruce-Banner"
>>> A1
{'iron-man': 'Tony', 'CA': 'Steve', 'BW': 'Natasha', 'hulk': 'Bruce-
Banner'}
>>> A2
{'iron-man': 'Tony', 'CA': 'Steve', 'BW': 'Natasha', 'hulk': 'Bruce-
Banner'}
>>> CW
{'iron-man': 'Tony', 'CA': 'Steve', 'BW': 'Natasha'}
>>>
```

We have changed the A1 dictionary and the changes would also be reflected by A2 since both hold the same memory address, whereas CW holds a different dictionary. Consider that you have a dictionary and you want to access a key, which does not exist in the dictionary. The interpreter shows KeyError as follows:

```
>>> A1 = {'iron-man': 'Tony', 'CA': 'Steve', 'BW': 'Natasha', 'hulk':
'Bruce-Banner'}
>>> A1["panther"]
Traceback (most recent call last):
 File "<pyshell#1>", line 1, in <module>
 A1["panther"]
KeyError: 'panther'
>>>
```

In the preceding code, you can clearly see the error. If this happens in running code, your code will not get fully executed. In order to deal with this situation, we will use the get() method.

get()

The syntax of the `get()` method is as follows:

```
dict.get(key, default=None)
```

The `get()` method is used to get the value of a given `key` from the dictionary. If `key` is not found, then the default value or message will return. See the following example, where `key` is present:

```
>>> A1 = {'iron-man': 'Tony', 'CA': 'Steve', 'BW': 'Natasha', 'hulk':
'Bruce-Banner'}
>>> A1.get('iron-man',"not found")
'Tony'
```

In the preceding example, since the key is found, the custom message, not found, does not get printed. Let's see another example:

```
>>> A1.get('panther',"not found")
'not found'
>>> A1.get("Black")
>>>
```

If the custom message is not set, then nothing will be returned. There is another method, `setdefault()`, which is very much similar to the `get()` method with a little different functionality. Let's discuss the method with examples.

setdefault()

The syntax of `setdefault()` is as follows:

```
dict.setdefault(key1, default=None)
```

`key1` -- This is `key` to be searched.

Default -- if `key1` is not found, then the message will be returned and added to the dictionary. Let's see the following example:

```
>>> port1.setdefault(23, "Unknown")
'Telnet'
>>> port1
{80: 'http', 22: 'SSH', 23: 'Telnet'}
>>> port1.setdefault(19, "Unknown")
```

```
'Unknown'
>>> port1
{80: 'http', 19: 'Unknown', 22: 'SSH', 23: 'Telnet'}
```

If the message has been not been set, then it returns and adds a default value, None. See the following example:

```
>>> port1.setdefault(18)
>>> port1
{80: 'http', 18: None, 19: 'Unknown', 22: 'SSH', 23: 'Telnet'}
>>>
```

To avoid KeyError, we can use the get() method, but we can add one more check to avoid KeyError. The has_key() method facilitates you to check whether the given key exists or not.

has_key()

The syntax for has_key() is given as:

```
dict.has_key(key)
```

key--this is the key to be searched in the dictionary, dict. The has_key() method returns True or False, as shown in the following example:

```
>>> port1 = {80: 'http', 18: None, 19: 'Unknown', 22: 'SSH', 23: 'Telnet'}
>>> port1.has_key(80)
True
>>>
>>> port1.has_key(20)
False
>>>
```

Consider a situation where you want to do some operation on a dictionary's keys and want to get all the keys in different lists. In this situation, you can use the keys() method.

keys()

The syntax of keys() is as follows:

```
dict.keys()
```

Let's consider the following example:

```
A1 = {'iron-man': 'Tony', 'CA': 'Steve', 'BW': 'Natasha', 'hulk': 'Bruce-
Banner'}
```

In the preceding dictionary, we want the superhero's characters, that is, all the keys:

```
>>> A1 = {'iron-man': 'Tony', 'CA': 'Steve', 'BW': 'Natasha', 'hulk':
'Bruce-Banner'}
>>> A1.keys()
['iron-man', 'CA', 'BW', 'hulk']
>>>
```

The preceding method returns a list of all the keys.

Similarly, if we want all the values in a separate list, we can use the `values()` method.

values()

The syntax of `values()` is as follows:

```
dict.values()
```

Let's consider the following example:

```
A1 = {'iron-man': 'Tony', 'CA': 'Steve', 'BW': 'Natasha', 'hulk': 'Bruce-
Banner'}
```

In the preceding dictionary, we want to get all the real names of our heroes:

```
>>> A1 = {'iron-man': 'Tony', 'CA': 'Steve', 'BW': 'Natasha', 'hulk':
'Bruce-Banner'}
>>> A1.values()
['Tony', 'Steve', 'Natasha', 'Bruce-Banner']
>>>
```

Dictionary to another dictionary. Consider the following example: Sometimes, we need to add one dictionary to another dictionary. Consider the following example:

```
port1 = {22: "SSH", 23: "telnet", 80: "Http"}
```

We have another dictionary of ports, that is, `port2` as shown:

```
port2 = {53 :"DNS", 443 : "https"}
```

In order to update `port1` with `port2`, we can take advantage of the `update()` method.

update()

The syntax is given as:

```
dict.update(dict2)
```

`dict2`--this is the dictionary to be added.

Consider the following example:

```
>>> port1 = {22: "SSH", 23: "telnet", 80: "Http" }
>>>
>>> port2 = {53 :"DNS", 443 : "https"}
>>>
>>> port1.update(port2)
>>> port1
{80: 'Http', 443: 'https', 53: 'DNS', 22: 'SSH', 23: 'telnet'}
>>>
```

Be careful to use the preceding method because if `dict` and `dict2` dictionaries contain the same key, then the `dict` dictionary's keys would be replaced by the keys of the `dict1` dictionary.

items()

The syntax of the `items()` method is as follows:

```
dict.items()
```

The `items()` method returns the list of dictionary's `(key, value)` tuple pairs:

```
>>> dict1 = d={1:'one',2:'two',3:'three'}
>>> dict1.items()
[(1, 'one'), (2, 'two'), (3, 'three')]
>>>
```

Sometimes, we need to delete all the items of a dictionary. This can be done by using the `clear()` method.

clear()

The syntax of `clear()` is as follows:

```
dict.clear()
```

Let's consider the following example:

```
>>> dict1={1:'one',2:'two',3:'three'}
>>> dict1
{1: 'one', 2: 'two', 3: 'three'}
>>> dict1.clear()
>>> dict1
{}
>>>
```

Python dictionary with for loop

In this section, we will learn how to use the for loop with a dictionary. If you have not read about the for loop so far, you can skip this section and get back after learning about the for loop, covered in Chapter 6, *Control Statements and Loops*. Let's apply the for loop to a dictionary. See the following program named forloopkey.py:

```
port1 = {21: "FTP", 22 :"SSH", 23: "telnet", 80: "http"} for each in port1:
print each
```

The output is as follows:

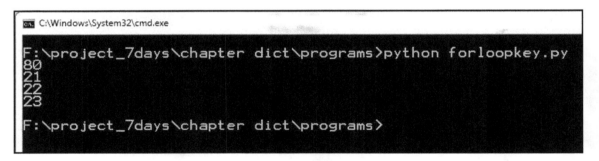

Output of program forloopkey.py

The preceding program prints only the keys of the dictionary. If you want to print the key as well as the value, then you can use the items() method. See the following program named forloopitems.py:

```
port1 = {21: "FTP", 22 :"SSH", 23: "telnet", 80: "http"}
for k,v in port1.items():
    print k," : ", v
```

The following screenshot shows the output of the program:

Output of program forloopitems.py

The preceding program seems difficult to understand at first. Let's break the program into two parts. The `port1.items()` method returns a list of tuple pairs, as shown:

```
>> port1 = {21: "FTP", 22:"SSH", 23: "telnet", 80: "http"}
>>> port1.items ()
[(80, 'http'), (21, 'FTP'), (22, 'SSH'), (23, 'telnet')]
>>>
```

The `for` loop sends each tuple to the variables, `k` and `v`. See the one iteration of `for` loop:

```
>> k,v = (80, 'http')
>>> k
80
>>> v
'http'
>>>
```

Now, you have learned how to iterate through a dictionary. Consider a dictionary of millions of items, and you want to iterate through the dictionary. The `items ()` method returns a list of key-value pairs. The newly created list will also take a lot of memory. A Python dictionary has a very beautiful memory-saving method called `iteritems()`. Let's understand it by the following example code named `forloopiter.py`:

```
port1 = {21: "FTP", 22 :"SSH", 23: "telnet", 80: "http"} for k,v in
port1.iteritems(): print k," : ", v
```

See the output:

Output of forloopiter.py program

The preceding code does not create a list. Let's understand by Python shell:

```
>> port1 = {21: "FTP", 22 :"SSH", 23: "telnet", 80: "http"} >>>
port1.iteritems() <dictionary-itemiterator object at 0x02A66210> >>>
```

The preceding code returns a dictionary object, not a huge list. We will not delve into the details of the object. You can replace `key()` by `iterkeys()` and `values()` by `itervalues()`. When to use `iteritems()` and `items()` ? If we need the corresponding list and have to do some operations on the list, such as slicing and indexing, then the `items()` method will be the most suitable. But if our need is just to iterate through the dictionary, then `iteritems()` will be the most suitable.

Practical program

Let's make some program to understand the dictionary. Make a dictionary from two lists. Both the lists are of equal length. Take the lists as shown:

```
list1 = [1, 2, 3, 4, 5]
list2 = ["a", "b", "c","d", "e"]
```

The `list1` values act as the keys of the dictionary and the `list2` values act as the values. The following is the program for it:

```
list1 = [1, 2, 3, 4, 5]
list2 = ["a", "b", "c","d", "e"]
dict1 = {}
for index1 in xrange(len(list1)):
  dict1[list1[index1]] = list2[index1]
print dict1
```

The output is as follows:

```
C:\Windows\System32\cmd.exe

F:\project_7days\chapter dict\programs>python excecisedict1.py
{1: 'a', 2: 'b', 3: 'c', 4: 'd', 5: 'e'}

F:\project_7days\chapter dict\programs>
F:\project_7days\chapter dict\programs>
```

Output of exercise 1

Let's do the preceding exercise in one line:

```
>>> list1 = [1,2,3,4,5]
>>> list2 = ["a", "b", "c","d", "e"]
>>> dict1 = dict([k for k in zip(list1,list2)])
>>> dict1
{1: 'a', 2: 'b', 3: 'c', 4: 'd', 5: 'e'}
>>>
```

Just a one-liner code can make a dictionary from two lists. So, in the preceding example, we used the zip() function; zip() is a built-in function, which takes two lists and returns a list of two tuples, such as [(key, value)]. Let's see an example of the zip() function:

```
>> list1 = [1,2,3]
>>> list2 = ["a","b","c"]
>>> zip(list1, list2)
[(1, 'a'), (2, 'b'), (3, 'c')]
>>>
```

Exercise

1. Find the number of ways to find whether a key exists in a dictionary or not.
2. Use the dictionary, port1 = {21: "FTP", 22:"SSH", 23: "telnet", 80: "http"}, and make a new dictionary in which keys become values and values become keys, as shown: Port2 = {"FTP":21, "SSH":22, "telnet":23, "http": 80}

Summary

In this chapter, you learned about dictionaries, how to create an empty dictionary, adding items to the dictionary, and accessing and deleting values from a dictionary. In order to find the number of items in a dictionary, we used the `len()` function. There are other useful functions, such as `max()` and `min()` to find the maximum and minimum values in a dictionary, respectively. In dictionary methods you learned different methods, such as `copy()`, `keys()`, and `items()`. By using `items()`, we can iterate through a dictionary. In the end, you learned two memory-saving methods: `iteritems()` and `iterkeys()`.

6
Control Statements and Loops

In this chapter, we will understand the principles and working of different control statements, namely, `if`, `if...else`, and `if...elif...else`. We will also be understanding the principles and working of various loops, namely, the `for` and `while` loops. We will also get acquainted with the `xrange` function and statements such as `break`, `continue`, and `pass`.

Control statements

Now, most of the beginners must be wondering what are control statements. Control statements are nothing but a series of statements that a program follows to get the desired results. Let's first try to understand what are control statements and why they form an essential part of any programming language. You might have used the ATM machine to withdraw money. What do you do when you insert your debit card? The very first thing you watch on the screen are the options to chose from the menu. Now you have to perform certain actions, else your card would be turned away after some time, in case you keep the computer waiting for a long time. When you choose to withdraw, you have to provide the correct amount, which is required to be withdrawn from the machine. If you provide the wrong amount, the computer will immediately give the message "Please enter the correct amount". What happened here? Did you notice? Here computer is merely following instructions. It has been ordered to accept only the correct amount and prompt an error message on input of the wrong amount. This is one such scenario where you can see the use of control statements.

The if and if...else statement

If can be understood as metaphorical English *what if* which most people use in their day to day life. What if this doesn't happen? If I were to become a billionaire. If this match is drawn we are out of the champions' league. If Churchill had not come to power Battle of Britain would have been lost. If this car doesn't start, use the other one. We are loaded with numerous examples from across the globe on usage of *if*. Same is the case with programming languages. Majority of the programming languages have control statements and you will find majority of them use the keyword `if` in their control statements. Python is no different and also facilitates the usage of if. Let's understand with an example:

```
password= raw_input("Enter the passwordt")
if password=="MI6":
    print "Welcome Mr. Bond."
```

For entering inputs through command line `raw_input()` function is used in Python.

Any function or control statement block in Python is started by placing the colon at the end of the line. Colon here marks the beginning of the `if` block and `print` statement begins after one tab space right after the colon. Programmers usually make a mistake by mixing space with tab right after the colon.

In the preceding example, after password is entered, the interpreter checks for the entered string and compares with `"MI6"`; if password entered is correct, it prints `Welcome Mr. Bond.`. If the password is wrong, it will skip the `if` block and terminate the program:

```
C:\windows\system32\cmd.exe

C:\pydev\chapter 6\code>python if_block.py
Enter the password     MI6
Welcome Mr. Bond.

C:\pydev\chapter 6\code>
```

But merely using only if doesn't give much of the choice to the interpreter and it has to terminate the program. What if the interpreter is given an alternative for a failed if test. In that case, else can be used to give choice to the interpreter.

Syntax

```
if condition :
        statements-1
else:
        statements-2
```

Let's take an example to understand if and else conditions:

```
password= raw_input("Enter the passwordt")
if password=="MI6":
    print "Welcome Mr. Bond."
else:
    print "Access Denied."
```

Here, if the password is entered wrongly, the interpreter will immediately execute statement inside the else block. Here, the control statement is divided into two blocks one is the if block and the other is the else block. At one time, the interpreter will execute either of the two blocks:

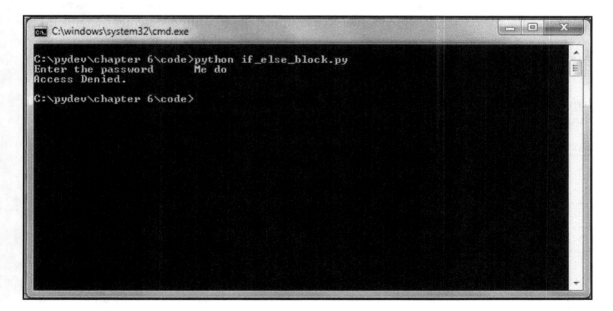

The if...elif...else statement

If there are a series of actions to be executed, then the if...elif...else block can be used. Most of the programming languages provide the if...else if...else control block, while Python has shortened else if to elif but the principle remains the same, that is, it divides the complete control block into number of blocks for specific action to be executed. It can be interpreted with day-to-day examples, for example, if this debit card doesn't work, use this credit card, else pay with a cheque.

Syntax

```
if condition-1:
        sequence of statements-1
elif condition-n:
        sequence of statements-n
else:
        default sequence of statements
```

Here, in the syntax, we are illustrating a series of branching statements under different conditions which is also called **conditional branching** in any language. First, we encounter an if block and if the condition inside the if block is satisfied or becomes true, only then will the if block be executed. If while executing the condition inside the if block is not satisfied, then the control is handed over to the immediate condition statement, that is, elif block, where the condition would be checked differently, and, finally, we have the else block, where if all the conditions before the else condition fail, then the else block will process the code.

Now, let's try to put college grades into use and understand how we can put the grades through programming:

Grade	Score
A	All grades above 4
B	All grades above 3 and below 3.5
C	All grades above 2.5 and below 3
D	All grades below 2.5

```
num =float(raw_input("Enter the number:"))
```

```
if num > 4:
        letter = 'A'
elif num > 3:
         letter = 'B'
elif num > 2:
         letter = 'C'
else:
         letter = 'D'
print "The Grade is " , letter
```

Here we have declared a variable num to store the marks entered and we have created a set of conditions, which will check the marks input. For example, if the marks entered are greater than 4, then the code inside the if condition would be executed and the letter variable would be assigned the value 'A' or grade A. Likewise, if the marks entered are less than or equal to 4, but greater than 3, then the if condition would fail and the control will be passed onto the elif num>3 conditional block and the letter variable would be assigned the value of 'B' or the grades B would be assigned to the entered marks. Here, the interpreter checks for the entered input and executes the correct block as per the correct marks entered. We entered marks 4.5 and the interpreter gives us grade A as shown in the following screenshot:

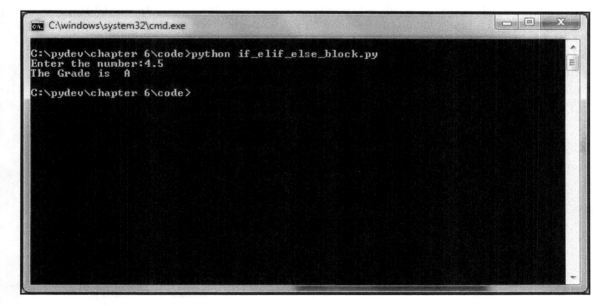

Loops

There might be a situation where you might require to run a single block of code a number of times, in that situation, loops come in handy. Loops come handy in situations such as iterating through data structures in any programming language or traversing through large sets of data to filter out junk data, followed by certain keywords followed by alphanumeric characters followed by certain special characters.

Types of loops

There are two types of loops, namely:

1. **Definite**: In this case, the code of block runs for a defined number of times. This is useful when the programmer exactly knows in how many counts the task will be executed or let's assume that he knows the number of elements inside the data structure. For example, the strength of a classroom.

2. **Indefinite**: In this case, the code of block runs until the condition is true. This is useful where the count is unknown. For example, trying to figure out the number of times London appears in a literary article.

Before further delving into loops, let's try to understand the `range()` and `xrange()` functions in Python.

The `range()` function comes handy when you want to generate a list on-the-fly. Its syntax is as follows:

Syntax

```
range(start-value, end-value, difference between the values)
```

```
C:\windows\system32\cmd.exe - python

C:\pydev>python
Python 2.7.13 (v2.7.13:a06454b1afa1, Dec 17 2016, 20:42:59) [MSC v.1500 32 bit (
Intel)] on win32
Type "help", "copyright", "credits" or "license" for more information.
>>>
>>>
>>>
>>> range(10)
[0, 1, 2, 3, 4, 5, 6, 7, 8, 9]
>>>
>>>
>>> range(2,10)
[2, 3, 4, 5, 6, 7, 8, 9]
>>>
>>> range(2,10,3)
[2, 5, 8]
>>>
>>>
```

Here, range(10) will generate a list, which has elements starting from 0 upto 9.
range(2,10) means the list will be generated starting from 2 and will have elements
upto 9. The range(2,10,3) means the list will be generated starting with 2 and having a
difference of 3 after each element.

Syntax

```
xrange(start-value, end-value, difference between the values)
```

 The xrange() is quite similar to range() except that xrange() releases or
frees the memory when not in use, whereas range() doesn't release the
memory.

Definite loop

It is a loop which is executed a set number of times. The best example that can be thought of
a definite loop is a for loop. Let's take a look at the for loop:

Syntax

```
for <variable> in xrange(<an integer expression >):
        <statement-1 >
        <statement-n >
```

The first line of code in the `for` loop is sometimes called the **loop header**. An integer expression specifies the number of times the loop has to run. The colon : ends the loop header. Python's `for` loop block or body consists of the statements below the header that will be executed a set number of times. The `for` loop body must be indented. The statements inside the loop body are executed sequentially on each run.

Let's try some example:

```
for a in xrange(4):
    print "Hello all"
```

Here, in the preceding example, we are trying to print "`Hello all`" four times.

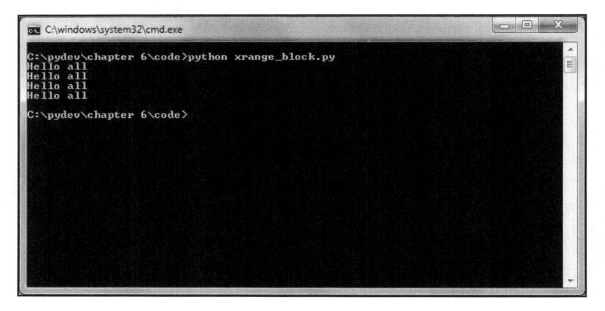

Here, a is any variable or iterating variable or counter variable whose initial value is 0 and will execute 4 times. Let's take another example:

```
for count in xrange(4):
    print count
```

Here the value of `count` will be printed one at a time and always on a new line.

In the preceding examples, the output is printed on a new line, but the output can be formatted to be printed in one line. For this, comma or , can be used as shown:

```
for count in xrange(4):
    print count,
```

The use of , will give you an output similar to this:

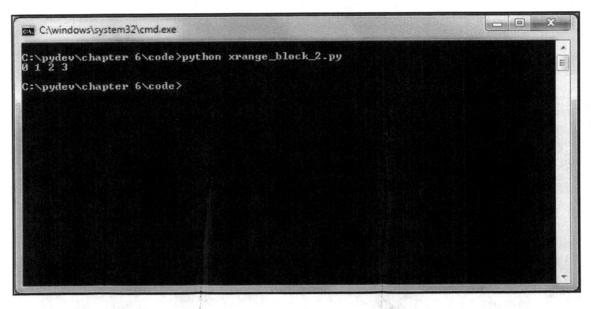

Let's consider some more examples:

```
product =1
for count in xrange(1,5):
    product = product*count
    print product,
```

We are interested to print the product times count. For this, we create a variable product whose value we initialize with 1 and generate a list of numbers from 1 to 5, but not including 5. For one iteration of the for loop, the product is multiplied the number of times the count value.

Here, the `count` value is nothing but the numbers from our list. We will be getting an output as shown here:

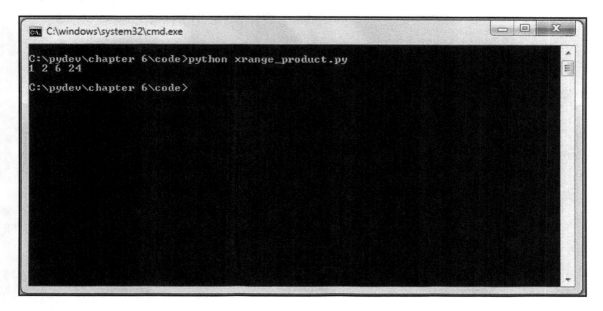

Let's take another example of the `for` loop. Here, we are interested in printing each character in a given string:

```
for each in 'VIENNA PHILHARMONIC' :
    print each,
```

For every single iteration of the `for` loop variable, `each` will store the value of every single character and will print them one by one in a single line, as shown here:

```
C:\windows\system32\cmd.exe

C:\pydev\chapter 6\code>python for_block_1.py
V I E N N A    P H I L H A R M O N I C

C:\pydev\chapter 6\code>
```

Indefinite loop

So far we learned about definite loop, now we will understand what is an indefinite loop? Indefinite loop is a loop that will continue to run infinite number of times until and unless it is asked to stop. In order to execute an indefinite loop, we use the `while` statement.

Syntax

```
while <condition>:
        <statements>
```

This loop will continue to execute until the condition is met and will terminate once the condition is not met. Let's try to understand with an example:

```
checking_acc = 5678143
num = int(raw_input("Enter the account numbert"))
while checking_acc != num:
```

```
        print "Wrong number "
        num = int(raw_input("Enter the right account numbert"))
    print "n*********"
    print "Your account number is" , num
```

Here, we are interested to validate a checking bank account. We take a variable `checking_acc`, which stores the value of a checking bank account. We take input from the user for his/her checking bank account number and store it in the `num` variable. We check the condition in the `while` loop and compare the input entered with our existing record of checking bank account. Here, until the correct account number is entered, the condition will keep on failing. So, in our case, if checking account is falsely entered, the user will get the message `Wrong number` and will be prompted to enter the correct number. Once he enters the correct number, the condition becomes true and the `while` loop terminates. You can see the output here:

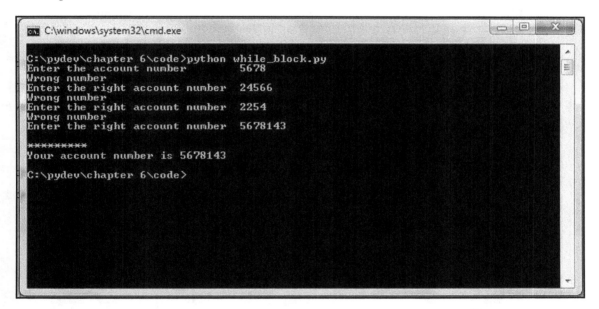

But there is a little tweak with which the `while` loop can be used and made to behave like a definite loop. Let's try to understand with an example:

```
sum = 0
  for counter in xrange(1,10):
      sum = sum+counter
      print sum,
      print "n"
  sum = 0
  counter = 1
```

```
while (counter < 10):
    sum = sum + counter
    print sum,
    counter= counter + 1
```

In our previous example, either the condition needs to be failed or it needs to be passed for the `while` loop to terminate. But if we insert a condition inside the `while` loop in such a manner that it will run for that definite time, then we can make the `while` loop to behave like a definite loop. In the preceding example, we are interested to print the sum of numbers from 1 to 10. We are achieving the same result using the `for` loop as well, when using the `while` loop. The `for` loop is simple and self-explanatory. To achieve similar results, we create a `counter` variable just before the `while` loop and initialize the variable with the value of 1. Now, until the value of `counter` is less than 10, it will continue to execute. Inside the `while` loop, we will increment the value of `counter` by 1 for every iteration. Thus, the loop will run only 10 times and on the tenth iteration, it will terminate. In the succeeding screenshot, the output of the `for` loop is displayed one by one on a new line, while the output of the `while` loop is displayed in a single line to differentiate the execution of both the loops (that is, `for` and `while`):

Both the `for` loop and `while` loop produce the same outcome. But the `while` loop block is a bit large, containing extra statements. The `counter` is the loop control variable, which must be explicitly initialized before the loop header. The `while` loop requires extra effort to make it work as a definite loop, but there would be several situations where the `while` loop will be the only solution available at hand.

The while True and break statement

Execution of an infinite `while` loop can be broken by the use of the `break` statement. Let's understand with an example:

```
sum = 0
while True:
    data = int(raw_input("Enter the data or press 0 to quit :"))
    if data == 0:
        break
    sum = sum+data
print "Sum is ", sum
```

Here we intend to print the sum of numbers being entered. In the preceding example, the `while` loop condition has been set to be Boolean, that is, `True`. In this case, the `while` loop will continue to execute infinitely as the condition will always be true. However, we can break this loop by setting up a condition check inside the `while` loop and then using a `break` statement. So, the loop will continue to run until the user keeps on entering numbers, but it will terminate as soon as the number 0 is entered. Here, once 0 is entered, the `if` condition inside the `while` loop will check and as the number entered is 0, the code inside the `if` block will execute, which is a `break` statement. This will terminate the loop and print the sum of the numbers entered as shown here:

Here, the `while` loop has Boolean value `True`, which is an entry condition for the `while` loop. In this case, the loop would execute at least once. But there is another way to achieve the preceding outcome without using the `break` statement. Let's have look at another example:

```
sum = 0
flag = 1
while flag == 1:
    data = int(raw_input("Enter the number or press 0 to quit :"))
    if data == 0:
        flag =0
    sum = sum+data
print "Sum is ", sum
```

We have achieved the same output without using the `break` statement. Here, we have used a `flag` variable instead of a `break` statement:

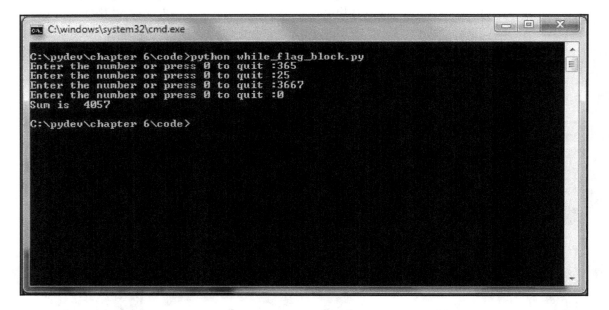

The initial entry point of the `while` loop is the value of the `flag` variable as 1. Until the `flag` variable is 0, the loop will continue to execute. When 0 is entered, the value of `flag` variable becomes 0 and the loop terminates.

The break statement

The break statements are used to change the flow of any block of statements. There might be a situation where we might need to break the loop in between; in that scenario, using the break statement will help us achieve our goal. Let's have a look:

```python
attraction_in_Vienna = ['Stephen plaz', 'Maria-Hilfer strasse', 'Donau-
insel', 'Vienna-Philharmonic']
first = "Donau-insel"
for each in attraction_in_Vienna:
    if(each == first):
        break
print each
```

Here we have created a list of attractions available in the city of Vienna. We take a variable first and assign it a value as "Donau-insel":

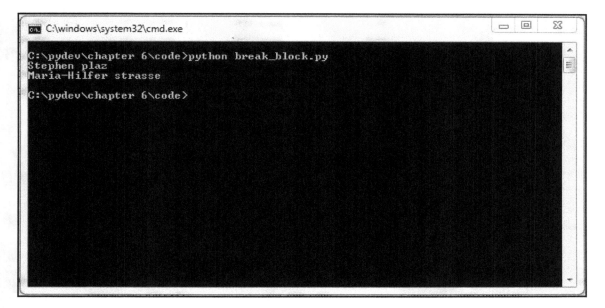

We want to print all the places of attraction in Vienna. But there is a twist. We would like to stop the moment `Donau-insel` occurs in the list. Hence, for every iteration of the `for` loop, the `if` block will check each and every element inside the list and compare it with the value we have given to compare, that is, `"Donau-insel"`. So the program will print all the names appearing before `Donau-insel`, and the moment `Donau-insel` occurs, the `break` statement terminates the loop. There can be several situations where the `break` statement can be handy such as searching for a keyword in a stack of words, searching a palindrome, and so on.

Nested loops

They are loops inside loops and there could be more than two loops each within another loop. In most situations, we generally use the `break` statement to break the inner loop while the outer loop will continue to execute. Let's try to understand its working with an example:

```
list1 = ["London","Paris","New York","Berlin"]
for each in list1:
 str1 = each
 for s in str1:
     if (s =="o"):
         break
     print s,
 print "n"
```

Here we are interested to print all the city's names and are not interested to print anything after character o. For this, we create a list of cities and we use the `for` loop to iterate through the list. We will use the second `for` loop to eliminate any characters appearing after character o. This condition is checked inside the second `for` loop, which is nested inside the first `for` loop with the help of the `if` statement:

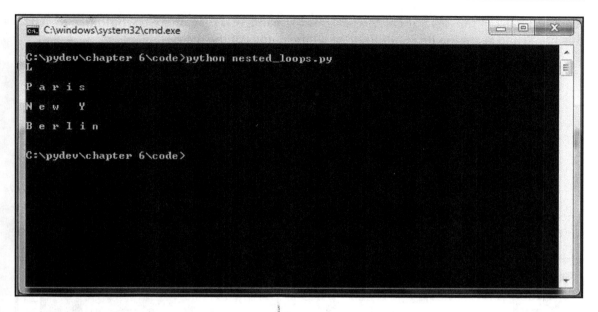

In this case, the inner loop breaks whenever char o is encountered, while the outer loop continues to execute.

The continue and pass statements

While the `break` statement terminates, the entire loop `continue` statement will skip that step and the loop will continue thereafter.

Let's discuss with an example:

```
movies = ['P.S I Love You', 'Shutter Island', 'Les Miserables play',
'King's Speech', 'Forest Gump']
```

Here is the list of movies but *Les Miserables* is the name of a play and we would like to skip this name and want the program to print all the names of the movies:

```
movies = ["P.S I Love You", "Shutter Island", "Les Miserables Play",
"King's Speech", "Forest Gump"]

for each in movies:
        if (each== "Les Miserables Play"):
                continue
        print each
```

The `for` loop iterates through each element of the list and the `if` block checks the condition for the occurrence of `"Les Miserables Play"`.

Here, the `continue` statement just skipped `"Les Miserables Play"` and the loop continued to print the rest of the names of the movies.

The pass statement

There can be scenarios in various programming problems, where you might want to reserve a loop for future use. We may not want to write anything inside the block, but at the same time the block cannot have an empty body. In this case, we use the `pass` statement to construct a body that does nothing.

Syntax

```
def fun():
        pass
for each in "Australia":
        pass
```

If you are wondering what is `def fun()`, it's nothing but defining the function with an empty body. In this case, the body does nothing:

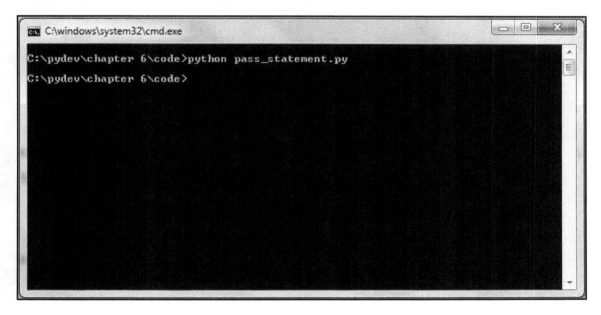

If you are wondering what functions are, then, do not worry, we will be covering them in a separate chapter on functions.

Summary

We started with understanding the concept of control statements and why they are essential in our day-to-day programming problems. We had a chance to look into two functions `range()` and `xrange()` that are used to generate a list on-the-fly. We learned about definite loops and indefinite loops. We also learned about the difference between definite and indefinite loops. Under definite loops, we learned about various control statements such as `if`, `if...else`, `if...elif...else`, and `for` loop. While, in indefinite loops, we had a chance to study the while statement and how we can also use the `while` loop to work as a definite loop. We saw the usage of while with the `break` statement and without the `break` statement. We also looked into the working of the `continue` and `pass` statements.

In the next chapter, we will learn about functions and scope of variables.

7
Function and Scope of Variable

In the previous chapter, we learned about control statements and loops. We learned about various types of control statements such as `if` statement, `if...else` statement, and `if...elif...else` statement. Next, we saw two main categories of loops, that is, definite and infinite loops. Under definite loops, we saw the working of for loop and we learned about two utility functions that are provided by Python, which can generate a list on-the-fly. They are `range()` and `xrange()`. Next, we learned about infinite loops, where we saw the working principle of the while loop. Then, we learned about nested loops along with break and continue statements. In this chapter, we will be covering functions, functions with arguments, functions with arguments and return value, functions with default arguments, functions with variable length arguments, key-value pairs as variable length arguments to the function, and finally we will be discussing on the scope of the variables.

Functions

The big question arising in the minds of the beginner would be, "What are functions?" and "Why are they necessary in any programming language?"

Functions are nothing but a small programming unit inside a big programming construct that generates a designated output. Let's try to understand with real-world scenario. It's difficult to think of a scenario where someone may not have access to television. What do you observe inside a normal television? On broader classification, considering a normal viewer, it has three functions:

- It has a display unit
- It has a volume control unit
- It has a channel tuning setup embedded inside the electronic circuitry

Although modern smart televisions have more complex functions, we will restrict our example to three main functions explained.

The display unit works differently from the other two functional units and its sole purpose is to put up a display to the user. Similarly, the volume control unit has its sole purpose to fine-tune the volume of the television, and, finally, channel tuning has the main function to have different channels loaded in the memory. Functions in programming language also work in a similar fashion, each has its own purpose defined. Some examples can be `calculateMonthSalary()`, `calculateTotalBill()`, and so on.

A method is an identical function in terms of name except that it is called on object and passed on the data, whereas a function is called directly by name and passed on the data to operate. A method is something that belongs to an object or in object-oriented programming class which contains the method. In this chapter, we will study more about functions.

Categories of functions

Functions in any programming language can fall into two broad categories:

- Built-in functions
- User-defined functions

Built-in functions

They are predefined by programming languages and each serves a specific purpose. While some built-in functions cannot be customized, some can be customized as per the programming guidelines laid down by a specific programming languages. The Python language also comes with a set of built-in functions such as `len()` and `cmp()`. You can get details about built-in functions from the Python documentation.

The Python documentation can be found at `https://docs.python.org`.

User-defined functions

They are defined by users as per their programming requirement. Functions can be created or can exist in various forms in any programming language. In this section, we will learn in depth about various ways in which we can create a function.

Function definition

There are some simple rules to define a function in Python. They are as follows:

- Use the `def` keyword followed by function name with parentheses `()`
- Any argument to the function must be placed within these parentheses `()`
- The code block must start with a colon `:`
- The code within the function must be indented

The syntax for this is as follows:

```
def function_name(arguments):
        <statements>
        return value
```

This is the syntax of any function definition in Python. If there are any arguments, they are written inside the parentheses and if the function has any return value that would be the last statement in any function code block or function body. The function code block or function body starts immediately after colon (:) and ends with return value if there is any return value. In Python, the body of any code block which starts after a colon (:) must be indented using spaces (preferably) or else with a tab. This eliminates indentation errors, which the interpreter might throw while running the program.

More on indentation is available at:
`https://www.python.org/dev/peps/pep-0008/#tabs-or-spaces.`

Next, we will see how to call a function in a program.

Calling a function

You might be wondering what is *calling a function*. Now, let's suppose you wrote some business logic about washing instructions to be embedded inside an automatic washing machine. Let's say you want to time sequence for rinsing of clothes immediately after wash. In programming language, you don't want to get lost writing a big chunk of program, so, in order to make things easy, you write your business logic inside a function. This function has to be called when you want that particular sequence to be timed right after the washing sequence finishes. There you pass the execution of instruction to the function written for timing of sequence. This is achieved by calling the function at an appropriate time.

Syntax block of code is:

```
function_name(arguments)
```

A function can be called within a programming construct similar to the built-in function. Use the name of the function followed by a set of parentheses. A function can be called any number of times within the same programming file, or another, or can be called within another function. Yes you got it right: a function can call another function. Let's learn from an example:

```
def helloWorld():
    """ This is Hello World Program"""
    print "You are in Hello World"

helloWorld()
```

Here, we define the `helloWorld()` function and we give a body, which has a comment and a print statement. Finally, we simply call the function by merely typing the name of the function followed by parentheses. When the program is run, we get the output as shown here:

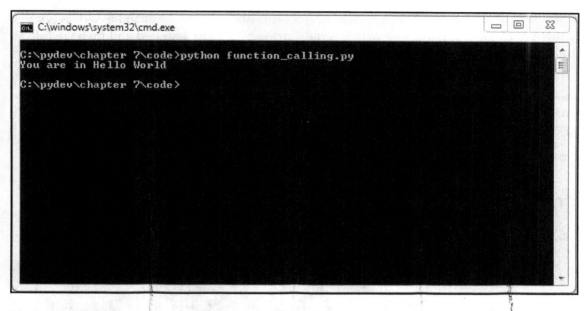

There are various ways in which a function can be written or exists in any programming language. We will discuss various ways in which a function can be formed in Python.

Function with arguments

So far we saw a function which had no arguments, now we will learn about functions with arguments. A function can contain any number of arguments depending on the business requirement. Let's try to understand with an example:

```
def func(passArgument):
    print passArgument
str = "hello all"
func(str)
```

In the preceding example, the `func` function accepts one argument which has a data type string. We create a variable `str` with a certain string statement assigned and then we call the `func` function and thereby pass the value of `str`. Finally, the output will look something like this:

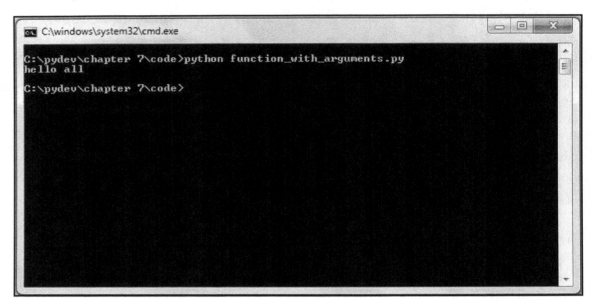

In the preceding example, what will happen if we do not pass any argument to the function?

```
def func(passArgument):
    print passArgument
str = "hello all"
func()
```

It will simply throw a `TypeError` as shown in the following screenshot:

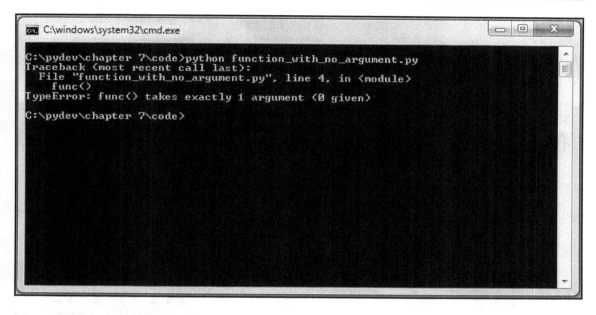

Hence, it becomes mandatory to pass an argument to the function during function calling after the function has been defined to accept arguments.

Function with an argument and return type

Sometimes, it may be necessary to return any specific datatype or value from a function which takes any arbitrary number of arguments. Let's evaluate this scenario with an example:

```
def sum(a, b):
    c = a+b
    return c
x = 10
y = 50
print "Result of addition ", sum(x,y)
```

Here, we define the function, which accepts two arguments and the body evaluates their sum with return type as value of the sum, which is denoted by the `return c` statement. We then call the function in the print statement and pass the value of variable x and variable y. This will give us the output as shown next:

```
C:\windows\system32\cmd.exe

C:\pydev\chapter 7\code>python function_with_argument_n_return_value.py
Result of addition  60

C:\pydev\chapter 7\code>
```

Function with default argument

Sometimes you will be presented with a condition where there has to be some value assigned to the argument, which will be called as the default argument. Let's try to understand with real-life scenario. Most of us fill in certain forms for job application online. Now, in the form, there is a section for gender selection. In this case, programmers have inserted a default value as female. By default your sex will be set to female if you do not specifically change this value. Same is the case with the function with default arguments. Let's try to understand this with a small code example:

```python
def info(name, age=50):
    print "Name", name
    print "age", age
info("John", age=28)
info("James")
```

Here, the `info` function takes two arguments `name` and `age`. The `age` is the argument with the default value `50`. In this case, during the calling of the `info` function, if `age` is not provided, then the function will set the value of `age` as `50`. We have called the `info` function twice. In the first call, we pass the value of `"John"` and `age` as `28`, while in the second call, we just pass the value of `name` as `"James"`. We will get output as shown here:

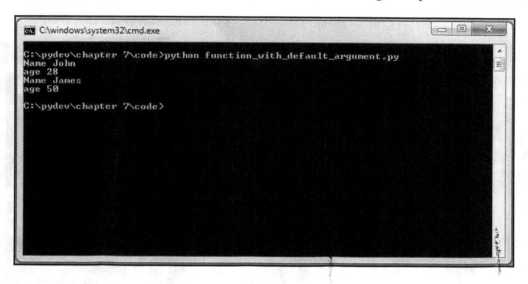

Function with variable length argument

There might be a scenario where you need to pass more arguments than specified during the function definition. In this case, variable length arguments can be passed:

Syntax
```
def   function_name(arg, *var):
        code block
        return
```

Here, `arg` means normal argument which is passed to the function. The `*var` refers to the variable length argument. This is will be more clear through the example:

```
def variable_argument( var1, *vari):
 print "Out-put is",var1
 for var in vari:
 print var
variable_argument(60)
variable_argument(100,90,40,50,60)
```

In this case, we define a function which takes two arguments, where the second argument is the variable length argument. When we call the function for the first time, we pass only 60 as the value to the argument and the function takes it as the first argument. During our second call to the function, we pass five numbers, so the function takes them as variable length argument. Depending on the nature of arguments passed, the function either considers the first argument or the variable length argument. Finally, we could see a different output based on our passing of different values as shown here:

```
C:\windows\system32\cmd.exe

C:\pydev\chapter 7\code>python function_with_variable_length.py
Out-put is 60
Out-put is 100
90
40
50
60

C:\pydev\chapter 7\code>
```

Key-value pair as variable length argument

Under certain circumstances, there might be a situation, where the key-value pair needs to be passed as the variable length argument to the function. Let's take one example here. In the given example, the key-value pairs are passed as variable length arguments:

```
def infocity(**var):
 print var
 for key, value in var.items():
 print "%s == %s" %(key,value)


infocity(name="14w", age = 20, city="Los Angeles")
infocity(name="John",age=45, city="London", sex="male", medals=0)
```

Using a for loop we print out each key-value pair that is passed to the function. On the first call, we pass only few key-value pairs, while in the second call to the function, we pass a bit more key-value pairs and we get the output as shown here:

```
C:\windows\system32\cmd.exe

C:\pydev\chapter 7\code>python function_with_key_value_pair_as_variable_length_a
rgument.py
{'city': 'Los Angeles', 'age': 20, 'name': '14w'}
city == Los Angeles
age == 20
name == 14w
{'city': 'London', 'age': 45, 'name': 'John', 'medals': 0, 'sex': 'male'}
city == London
age == 45
name == John
medals == 0
sex == male

C:\pydev\chapter 7\code>
```

Pass by reference versus pass by value

Pass by reference is the term used in some programming languages, where values to the argument of the function are passed by reference, that is, the address of the variable is passed and then the operation is done on the value stored at these addresses.

Pass by value means that the value is directly passed as the value to the argument of the function. In this case, the operation is done on the value and then the value is stored at the address.

In Python arguments, the values are passed by reference. During the function call, the called function uses the value stored at the address passed to it and any changes to it also affect the source variable:

```
def pass_ref(list1):
  list1.extend([23,89])
  print "list inside the function: ",list1
list1 = [12,67,90]
print "list before pass", list1
```

```
pass_ref(list1)
print "list outside the function", list1
```

Here, in the function definition, we pass the list to the `pass_ref` function and then we extend the list to add two more numbers to the list and then print its value. The list extends inside the function, but the change is also reflected back in the calling function. We finally get the output by printing out different representations of the list:

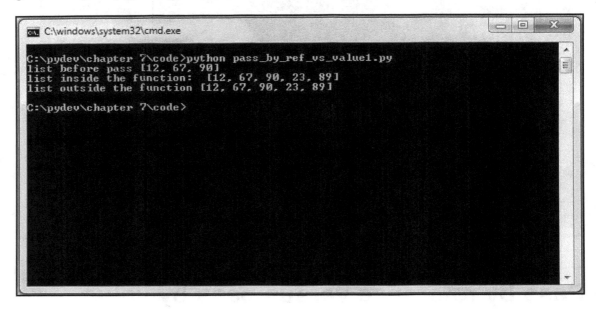

Let's look at another scenario:

```
def func(a):
  a=a+4
  print "Inside the function", a
a= 10
func(a)
print "Outside the function", a
```

The preceding example might make you think it is called by value, as the change happening inside the Python function does not get reflected back in the calling function. It is still a pass by reference, as, in this situation inside the function, we made new assignment, that is, a= a+4. Although you might think that a = a + 4 is changing the number stored in a, but it is actually reassigning a to point to a new value:

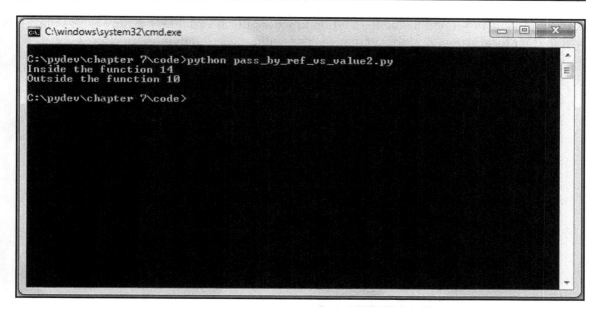

```
C:\windows\system32\cmd.exe

C:\pydev\chapter 7\code>python pass_by_ref_vs_value2.py
Inside the function 14
Outside the function 10

C:\pydev\chapter 7\code>
```

Scope of variables

This could be an intriguing topic for you to understand for the first time. But it is actually a very simple topic. Let's try to understand this with a real-life situation. You might be aware of two types of airlines: domestic and international carriers. The scope of domestic carriers will be restricted to a particular country's operation only, while an international carrier has the scope to operate on an international border. Same is the case with variables. The scope on the broader aspect defines the access level for specific variable. There are two basic scopes of variables in Python:

- Local variables
- Global variables

A local variable is defined inside the Python function. Local variables are only accessible within their local scope. A global variable is defined outside the Python function. Global variables are only accessible throughout the program:

```
1      k = 4
2
3    □def main():
4          list1 = []
5
6    □      def add():
7    □          for x in xrange(k):
8                  list1.append(x)
9              print list1
10
11         add()
12
13     main()
```

Here, the variable k with value 4 is an example of a global variable, while the list1 variable is an example of a local variable. The area marked in green inside the main() function shows the scope of the list1 variable, while the area marked in yellow shows the scope within the add() function, and this scope is valid until the end of the add() function.

The succeeding example will explain both these types of variables:

```
def func():
  a =12
  print '''Inside the function the value of
  a is acting as local variable''', a
a= 10
func()
print '''Outside function the value of a is
  acting as global variable''',a
```

Variable a is a global variable; its value remains the same outside the function compared to the value inside the function, where it is acting as a local variable:

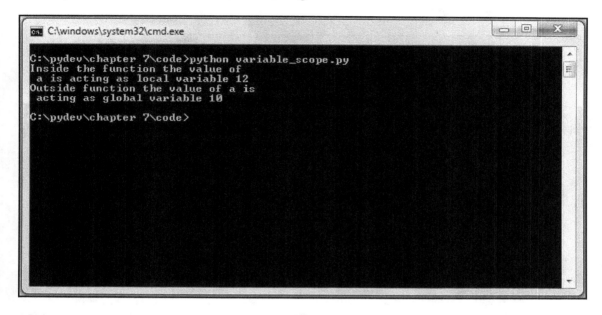

Let's analyze another situation:

```
def func():
 a =12
 print "a inside the function is the local variable",a
func()
print "Trying to access the local variable outside the function.",a
```

Here we have declared variable a whose scope is local to the `func()` function. As we try to access the local variable, the interpreter does not support us on this and will tell you something as shown next:

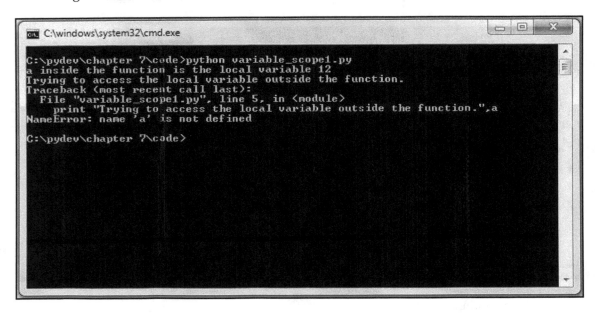

But this situation can be overcome using the `global` keyword, as we will use in our next example:

```
def func():
    global k
    k=k+7
    print "variable k is now global",k
k=10
func()
print "Accessing the value of k outside the function",k
```

In this case, we declare the k variable as global using the `global` keyword inside the function. We can now access it from anywhere. The `global` keyword tells the interpreter that the variable is global and it should stop searching across all the functions or local scopes.

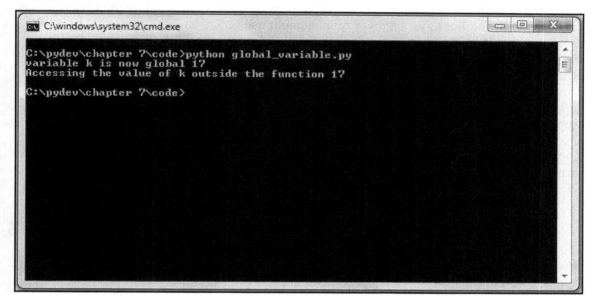

Memory management

This is quite a fascinating topic and is also a big pain for any programmer who has to deal with memory-related issues such as memory leakage issues. However, since it is a big topic which needs to be covered at the intermediate stage, we will try to explain the very basics of the topic. In the earlier days, memory management used to be handled manually by all the programmers. Who could better understand manual memory management than C/C++ language programmers. New and modern programming languages such as Java and others are coming loaded with more advanced memory management mechanism, so programmers have to worry less in this area as every issue is taken care by the language garbage collection facility. We have already covered what is local scope and what is global scope are. Local scope of the function, contains parameters and variables. The complete local scope must be stored somewhere in the RAM of the computer. Language divides the RAM into two parts called run-time stack and the heap. Memory is divided into two parts in any programming language:

- Stack or run-time stack
- Heap

The heap is a specific area of RAM where all values (objects) are stored. The run-time stack never contains the object. The run-time stack store only references pointing toward the values stored in the heap. Let's try to understand with an example:

```
line 1 :k = 4
line 2 :def main():
line 3 :   list1 = []
line 4 : def add():
line 5 :         for x in xrange(k):
line 6 :                  list1.append(x)
line 7 :         print list1
line 8 :   add()
line 9: main()
```

During execution of lines 5, 6, and 7 of the code, the run-time stack looks as shown in the next figure. There are three activation records present on run-time stack. The interpreter first puts the **module Activation Record**. While executing the module, the interpreter goes from top to bottom and places the variable definition of the module scope into the activation record of the module. The activation record of the module consists of the reference **k** to the value **4**.

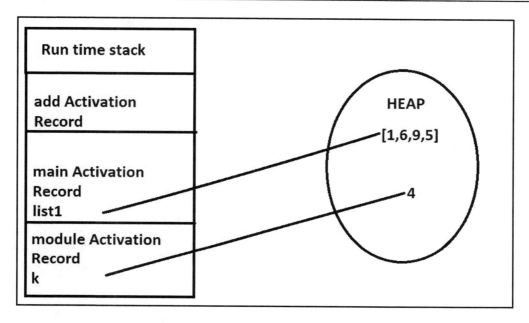

Summary

In this chapter, we learned about functions and how to define a function. Then we discussed various types of functions such as built-in and user-defined functions. We saw various examples of user-defined functions, where we explained functions with no arguments and no return type, functions with arguments, functions with arguments and return type, functions with default arguments, and functions with variable length arguments. We also learned about key-value pairs being passed as a variable length argument to the function. We came across the scope of the variable and, finally, we examined the basic concepts of memory management where we learned about two types of memory, namely, stack and heap.

In the next chapter we will learn about quite an interesting topic: collections.

8
Modules and Packages

In the previous chapter, you learned about the Python functions. In this chapter, you will learn the Python modules. A Python module is the Python source file, which can consist of statements, classes, functions, and variables.

Modules

Modules are code files meant to be used by other programs. In order to use a module, we use the `import` statement. A module can import other modules.

Let's discuss the simple Python program:

```
def sum1(a,b):
  c = a+b
  return c

def mul1(a,b):
  c = a*b
  return c
```

The preceding code is a very easy and basic example. Let's save the program as `module1.py`. You can consider that the preceding program is the Python module. We will use `module1.py`. Consider, while making another program, you need multiplication or addition of two numbers. You need not make any function. You can take the advantage of `module1.py`.

The import statement

In order to use the functions and variables of the `module1.py` program, we will use the `import` statement. The syntax of the `import` statement is shown here:

```
Import module1, module2, module
```

In this way, you can import multiple modules. Let's make another program `mod1.py`, which will import `module1.py`:

```
import module1
x = 12
y = 34
print "Sum is ", module1.sum1(x,y)
print "Multiple is ", module1.mul1(x,y)
```

As you know, the module contains statements and definitions and these statements and definitions are executed for the first time when the interpreter encounters the module name in the `import` statement.

In preceding code, the `module1` module gets executed when the interpreter encounters the `module1` name in the `import` statement. In order to use the module variables and functions, use the `module_name.variable` and `module_name.function()` notations. In the preceding code, we want to use the `sum1()` function of `module1`, that's why we use `module1.mul1()`.

Let's see the output:

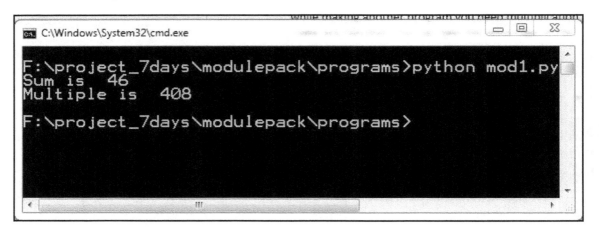

Output of the mod1.py program

If you think it is tedious and time consuming to write `module1` with every function of `module1.py`, then Python allows you to use the `as` statement as shown. The syntax is given as follows:

```
import module_name as new_name
```

Let's write a program `mod2.py`:

```
import module1 as md
x = 12
y = 34
print "Sum is ", md.sum1(x,y)
print "Multiple is ", md.mul1(x,y)
```

In the preceding code, `module1` is used as `md`. Let's see the output:

Output of the mod2.py program

You can explicitly define the function as per your need. Consider we want only the `sum1()` function not `mul1()`. Syntax is given as *module-name import function-name*

Let's write the code:

```
from module1 import sum1
x = 12
y = 34
print "Sum is ", sum1(x,y)
```

In the first line, I defined from where I am taking the `sum1()` function, then there will be no need to use `module1` with the function name. Let's see the output of the code:

Output of the mod3 program

Consider a module that contains many functions and you have to import all the functions. You can use the following statement as shown:

```
from module-name import *
```

But I advise you don't use the preceding statement because if you are importing more than one module, then it is very difficult to identify which function is taken from which module. Let's take an example. Consider one more module named as `module2`:

```
def sub1(a,b):
    c = a-b
    return c

def divide1(a,b):
    c = a/b
    return c
```

Now we have two modules `module1` and `module2`. We have defined `module1` earlier. Let's write the next program `mod4.py`:

```
from module1 import *
from module2 import *
x = 36
y = 12
print "Sum is ", sum1(x,y)
print "Substraction is ", sub1(x,y)
print "after divide ", divide1(x,y)
print "Multiplication is ", mul1(x,y)
```

In the preceding function, we imported all the functions of `module1` and `module2`. But it is very difficult to identify which function is coming from which module. The output of the program is as shown here:

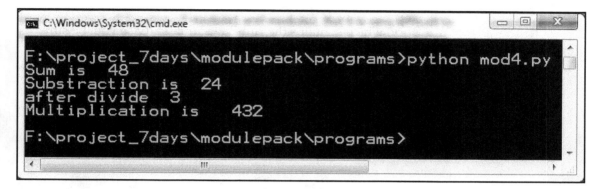

Output of the mod4 program

However, Python offers you the built-in function `dir()`, which can be used to identify the functions. See the example `mod5.py`:

```
import module1
print dir(module1)
```

The output of the program is as shown here:

The preceding is the output of the `mod5` program. After seeing the output, we can say that the `mul1()` and `sum1()` functions came from the `module1` module.

Locating Python modules

After encountering the `import` statement, the Python interpreter searches the module in the following sequence:

1. The current directory, which contains the running script. I advise you, be sure, that the name of your program is different from the importing modules.
2. `PYTHONPATH` has to be defined in the environment variable in Windows OS. Let's learn by example. Consider we move the `mod5.py` program to another directory as covered in the following screenshot.

   But the current directory does not contain any `module1` module. The output will be as shown here:

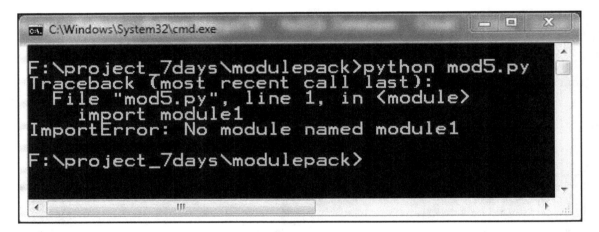

Output of mod5.py in a different directory

   We are running the `mod5.py` program from `F:project_7daysmodulepack`. The output shown there is no `module1` module found. Let's set the `PYTHONPATH` variable as shown here:

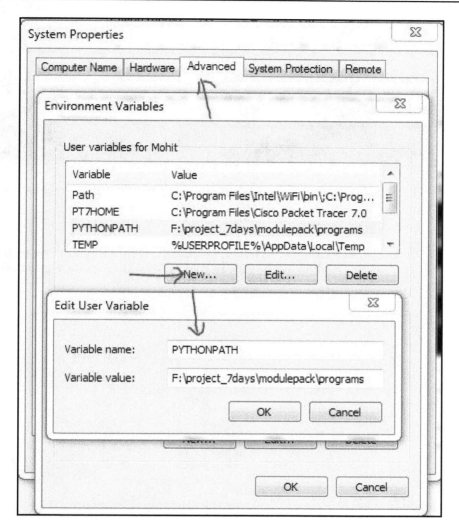

Setting the PYTHONPATH variable

After setting PYTHONPATH, you will have to reboot your computer. After reboot, start the program again.

The output will be as shown here:

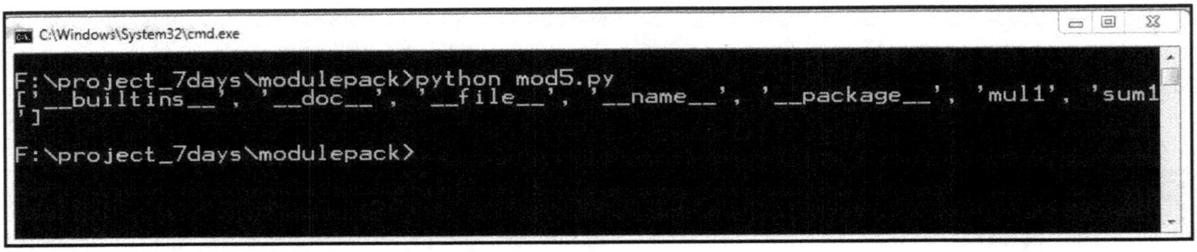

This is the output of the program after setting `PYTHONPATH`. Now you can see that there is no error, meaning the interpreter is able to find the `module1` module.

3. Here you have Python installed by default. If you want to know the installation path, you can check the `sys.path` variable in the `sys` module. Refer to the following example:

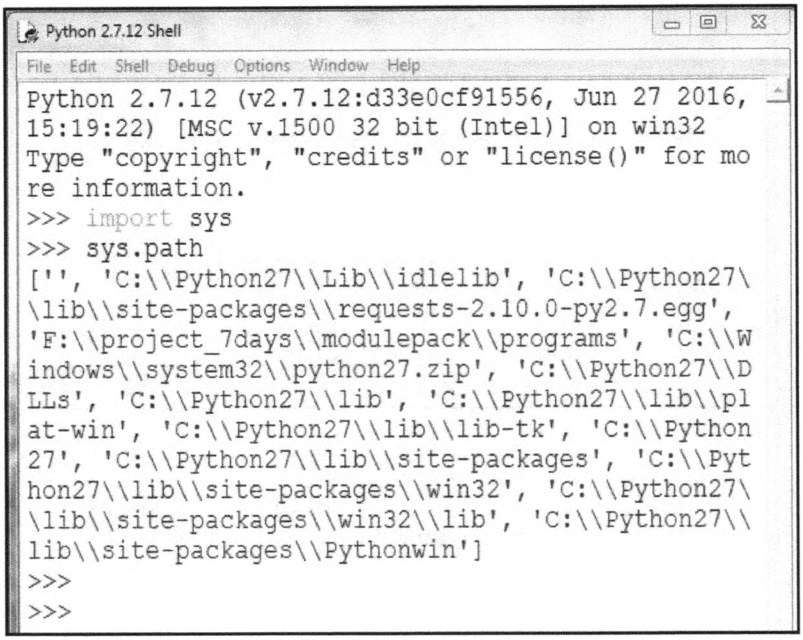

A screenshot showing sys path

The `sys.path` returns a list of default paths.

Compiled Python files

Whenever `module1.py` and `module2.py` are successfully compiled, an attempt is made to write the compiled version to `module1.pyc` and `module2.pyc` respectively. Refer to the following screenshot:

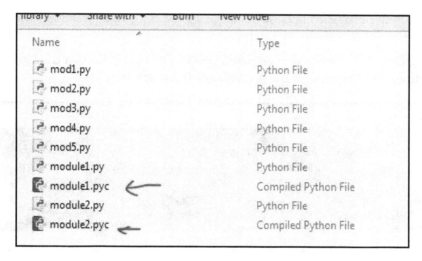

A screenshot showing the compiled files

The contents of the compiled file is platform independent, so a Python module can be used by machines on different architectures.

Let's discuss a special scenario, consider Bob make a program named `myprog.py` as shown:

```
def sum1(a,b):
    c = a+b
    return c
    print "Sum is ", sum1(3,6)
```

Let's run it:

Output of the myprog.py program

Bob's program is running successfully. Consider another user, Alice, who uses your program as a module.

Refer to Alice's program `alice1.py`:

```
import myprog
num = 10
total = num+myprog.sum1(23,12)
print "Alice total is ", total
```

The preceding program is very simple, just import `myprog.py` as a module and use the `sum1()` function of the `myprog` module. Let's see the output:

Output of the alice1.py program

The program is running successfully. With the output from `alice1.py` the output of `myprog.py` is also printed, which is unwanted. Any user who imports `myprog.py` as a module unwantedly would get the output of `myprog.py`. To avoid this situation, we made some amendments in `myprog.py`.

You can see the new version of program `myprog.py` here:

```
def sum1(a,b):
  c = a+b
  return c

if __name__ == '__main__' :
  print "Sum is ", sum1(3,6)
```

From the preceding code, what is the significance of __name__ and __main__. __name__ is a special variable that holds a string "__main__". If the program is being imported from another program, then __name__ would be set to the module's name.

Let's see the output of both the programs `myprog.py` and `alice1.py`:

Output of the myprog.py and alice1.py programs

If you are still not getting the point of the __name__ variable, let's discuss with examples. I have made temporary changes in the `myprog.py` program:

```
def sum1(a,b):
  c = a+b
  return c

print "name is ", __name__

if __name__ == '__main__' :
  print "Sum is ", sum1(3,6)
```

Let's run both the programs `myprog.py` and `alice1.py`:

Output of the myprog.py and alice1.py programs

So, in the preceding output, when `myprog.py` is being run, the __name__ variable returns a string value "__main__". Further, when `myprog` has been imported by another program as a module, then it returns a module named `myprog`. I hope everything is clear now.

The Python package

Python modules is a single file, whereas a Python package is a collection of modules. A package is a directory that contains Python modules and one additional file: `__init__.py`. What is the need of a package? Consider a team gets a project to convert the recording sound into MP3 format. One developer writes a code `rectomp3.py` to convert the recording voice to MP3 sound in the `sound_conversion` directory. After some time, the team gets new requirements to convert the recording voice to `.wav` format. Instead of writing in the `rectomp3.py` file, we write our own code `rectowav.py` file in `sound_conversion`. Then, a new requirement comes by where you need to convert the recording to WMA format. Again, a new author writes a new code `rectowma.py` file in the same directory `sound_conversion`. In this way, they make a package just adding one more file `__init__.py`. Let's take a practical example.

Here, you can see the code `rectomp3.py` in `sound_conversion`:

```
#Written by Mohit
def rec2mp3():
    """
    Converions code
    """
    return "recording voice converted to Mp3"
```

The preceding code is a dummy code, just for understanding. Let's see the second code `rectowav.py` in the same directory `sound_conversion`:

```
#Written by Bhaskar
def rec2wav():
    """
    Converions code
    """
    return"recording voice converted to wav"
```

The preceding code converts the recording voice to WAV format. Let's see the new code:

```
#Written by Denim
def rec2wma():
    """
    Converions code
    """
    return "recording voice converted to wma"
```

Now that all the code is written, make an empty file __init__.py in the directory
sound_conversion. The __init__.py file can be an empty file, but it can also be used to
import the module. Now our package is ready; let's import it. We will write a new program
voice_changer.py. Put the program outside the directory sound_conversion. Refer
to the program:

```
from sound_conversion import rectomp3
from sound_conversion.rectowma import rec2wma
print rectomp3.rec2mp3()
print rec2wma()
```

While executing the preceding file, the interpreter might give an error because the Python
interpreter doesn't know the sound_conversion path as shown.

Set the PYTHONPATH as shown here:

```
F:\project_7days\modulepack\programs>Set PYTHONPATH = F:\project_7days\modulepac
k\programs\sound_conversion

F:\project_7days\modulepack\programs>python voice_changer.py
recording voice converted to Mp3
recording voice converted to wma

F:\project_7days\modulepack\programs>
```

The preceding screenshot also shows that the code is running. If you want to create
voice_changer.py in another directory say F:/, let's copy and paste the code of
voice_changer.py in F:/ and run it. You might get an error if the interpreter is not able
to find the package as shown here:

```
E:\>python voice_changer1.py
Traceback (most recent call last):
  File "voice_changer1.py", line 1, in <module>
    from sound_conversion import rectomp3
ImportError: No module named sound_conversion

E:\>
```

An output showing error

In the preceding code, we are getting the error No module named sound_conversion, which means the interpreter did not get the package or module. Let's edit the code. Refer to the code shown here:

```
import sys
sys.path.append("F:project_7daysmodulepackprograms")
from sound_conversion import rectomp3
from sound_conversion.rectowma import rec2wma
print rectomp3.rec2mp3()
print rec2wma()
```

In the voice_changer1.py program, we edit the sys.path for the program using syntax sys.path.append("F:project_7daysmodulepackprograms"). Let's see the output:

Output of the voice_chnager1.py program

The preceding screenshot shows that the code is running successfully. In this way, you can load the package and modules.

Summary

In the *Module* section, you have learned how to make modules and how to import them. By using the dir() function, you can check the involved function in the modules. The Python package is a collection of modules: generally a Python package is a directory. You have learned how Python searches the modules and packages.

9
File Handling and Exceptions

So far you have seen the various Python programs, which took the input from the keyboard and delivered the output on the screen. In this chapter, you will, however, learn to take input from files and write result to the files. Also, we will go through the concept of exceptions.

Reading text from a file

In order to read and write into a file, we will use the `open()` built-in function to open the file. The `open()` function creates an `file_object` object. What is an object? You will understand in `Chapter 11`, *Class and Objects*. The Syntax is given as:

```
file_object = open(file_name ,access_mode)
```

The first argument,`file_name`, specifies the filename that you want to open. The second argument, `access_mode`, determines in which mode the file has to be opened, that is, read, write, append, and so on.

The read() method

Now we will read a file by a program. The access mode for reading is `r`.

Let's take the sample of a text file containing famous quotes:

```
1  Peace comes from within, Do not seek it without.
2  The mind is everything, What you think you become.
3  Nothing good ever comes of violence.
4  Life should be great rather than long.
5  Peace if possible, truth at all costs.
```
Sample file

I have saved the preceding file with the name `sample1.txt`.

Let's write a `readfile.py` program to read the earlier file:

```
file_input = open("sample1.txt",'r')
all_read = file_input.read()
print all_read
file_input.close()
```

In the given code, first we created a `file_input` file object, then we called `file_input.read()` to read the file content. After reading, the `file_input` file object is closed by `file_input.close()`. To be sure the sample file and the code `readfile.py` must be in the same directory. Let's check the output:

Reading a file

The preceding code is running successfully. In order to read character from the file, you can pass the argument to the `read()` function, for example, `read(5)` would read the first five characters of the file.

Let's understand the sample code `readcount1.py`:

```
file_input = open("sample1.txt",'r')
print file_input.read(20)
print file_input.read(15)
print file_input.read(10)
file_input.close()
```

Let's analyze the output:

Output of code read

The second line of code reads the first 20 characters of the file, the third line reads the next 15 characters, and the fourth line reads the next 10 characters of the file.

The readline() method

In order to read the file line by line, use `readline()`.

Let's see the sample code `readline1.py`:

```
file_input = open("sample1.txt",'r')
print file_input.readline()
print file_input.readline()
print file_input.readline()
file_input.close()
```

Let's see the output of code:

```
F:\project_7days\input_file\program>python readline1.py
Peace comes from within, Do not seek it without.

The mind is everything, What you think you become.

Nothing good ever comes of violence.

F:\project_7days\input_file\program>
```

In code, we have printed three lines. What happens, if you specify `count` in `readline(count)`. See the code `readlinecount.py`:

```
file_input = open("sample1.txt",'r')
print   file_input.readline(100)
print   file_input.readline(20)
file_input.close()
```

Let's see the output:

In the `file_input.readline(100)` syntax prints 100 characters of the first line. But the first line contains only 48 characters. The syntax `file_input.readline(20)` prints the 20 characters from the second line of `sample1.txt`.

The readlines() method

Consider the situation where you want to make a list of lines of a file; in that case, the `readlines()` method allows you to do that.

See the code in `readlines1.py`:

```
file_input = open("sample1.txt",'r')
print  file_input.readlines()
file_input.close()
```

Let's check the output of the code:

In the preceding screenshot, you can easily see the list of lines.

For reading purposes, you can loop over the file object. Let's analyze the code in `readfileforloop.py`:

```
file_input = open("sample1.txt",'r')
```

```
for line in file_input:
    print line
```

This is the output:

You can see all the lines. This is memory efficient, fast, and leads to simple code.

Exercise

Let's do an exercise.

See the given file, batman.txt, containing the quotes from famous Hollywood movies.

Our aim is to write a program to find a given word from the file:

```
1  Bruce Wayne: People are dying, Alfred
2  What would you have me do?
3  Alfred Pennyworth: Endure, Master Wayne.
4  Take it. They'll hate you for it,
5  but that's the point of Batman,
6  he can be the outcast.
7  He can make the choice that no one else can make,
8  the right choice.
9  The Batman didn't murder Harvey Dent.
```

Screenshot of batman.txt

Let's write a program to find the particular word from the file. We are making the assumption that the program should be case insensitive, which means it does not matter whether the characters are in uppercase or lowercase.

See the code in `findword.py`:

```
word = raw_input("Enter the word ")
word = word.lower()
file_txt = open("batman.txt", "r")
count = 0
for each in file_txt:
    if word in each.lower():
        count = count+1
print "The ", word ," occured ",count, " times"
```

The program is very easy to understand. Let's see the output of the code:

Output of findword.py

The program `findword.py` is working fine.

Writing text to a file

In this section, we will learn how to write a new file using Python.

This time we'll use the write mode `'w'` in `open()`. The `'w'` mode creates a new file. If the file already exists, then the file would be overwritten. We will use the `write()` function.

Let's discuss the code in `filewrite1.py`:

```
file_input = open("motivation.txt",'w')
file_input.write("Never give up")
file_input.write("nRise above hate")
file_input.write("nNo body remember second place")
file_input.close()
```

You can see that I have written the famous WWE star John Cena's quotes.

Let's see the output:

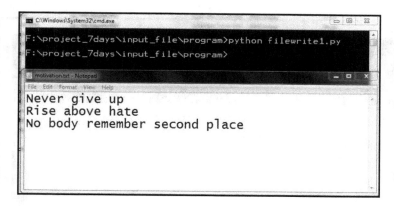

Output of code filewrite.py

We wrote lines one by one by adding a new line character n. You can supply all of them in one go as shown here:

```
file_input = open("motivation.txt",'w')
file_input.write("Never give up nRise above hate nNo body remember second
place")
file_input.close()
```

Next, I will use the `writelines()` function. This method writes a Python list of strings to a file.

Let's see the code:

```
list1 = ["Blood sweat and respectn",
  "The first two you given"
  "The last you earnn"
  "Give it Earn it"]
text_file = open("wwerockquotes.txt", 'w')
text_file.writelines(list1)
text_file.close()
```

In the preceding code, Python list, list1, contains some motivational lines, and we want to save that in a file. We could use the writelines() function for our requirement. Let's see the output:

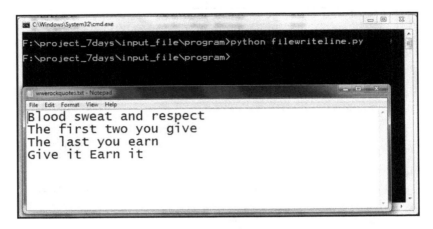

Output of filewriteline.py

Every time you run the program, the file gets overwritten, means a new file would be created. Consider the situation where you want to add content to the previous file; you can use access mode 'a'.

Let's use the preceding program filewritea.py with access mode 'a'.

```
file_input = open("newmotivation.txt",'a')
file_input.write("Never give up")
file_input.write("nRise above hate")
file_input.write("nNo body remember second place")
file_input.close()
```

Let's see the output:

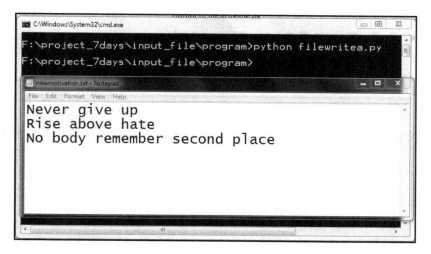

Output of filewritea.py

Let's run the program with different lines:

```
file_input = open("newmotivation.txt",'a')
file_input.write("nBlood sweat and respect")
file_input.write("nThe first two you give")
file_input.write("nThe last you earn")
file_input.write("nGive it Earn it")
file_input.close()
```

Let's see the output:

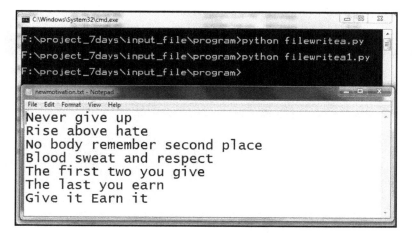

Output of program filewritea1.py

The `newmotivation.txt` file has been successfully appended.

There are other access modes too.

Examples

The `"r+"` opens a file for reading and writing. This mode places the pointer at the beginning of the file.

The `"w+"` opens a file for reading and writing. If the file doesn't exist, then a new file is created. If the file exists, then the file is overwritten.

The `"a+"` opens a file for appending and reading. If the file doesn't exist, it creates a new file. If the file already exists, the pointer is placed at the end of the file.

Pickling

Text files are convenient to use because you can read, write, and append them with any text editor, but they are limited to storing a series of characters. Sometimes you may want to store complex information such as list and dictionary. Here we would use Python's `pickle` module. The `pickle` module is used to store complex data such as list and dictionary. Let's discuss with the help of an example:

```python
import pickle
name = ["mohit","bhaskar", "manish"]
skill = ["Python", "Python", "Java"]
pickle_file = open("emp1.dat","w")
pickle.dump(name,pickle_file)
pickle.dump(skill,pickle_file)
pickle_file.close()
```

The program seems complex to understand. Let's understand the code line by line.

The `name` and `skill` are two lists which we have to store.

The `pickle_file = open("emp1.dat", "w")` syntax creates a `pickle_file` object in write mode as we have done earlier.

The `pickle.dump()` is used to dump and store the lists `name` and `skill` in the `pick.dat` file. The `pickle.dump()` requires two arguments, first the data (like list) to pickle and second the file to store it. The `pickle_file.close()` finally close the file. Let's see the output:

Output of pickle file

Now you must have an idea how to store complex data.

Unpickling

Unpickling means retrieving the data from the `pickle` file. In the previous topic, you learned how to store (`list`, `dictionary`) data in the `pickle` file; now it's time to retrieve the stored data. In order to perform unpickling, we will use `pickle.load()`. The `pickle.load()` takes one file object as an argument.

Let's see the program:

```
import pickle
pickle_file = open("emp1.dat",'r')
name_list = pickle.load(pickle_file)
skill_list =pickle.load(pickle_file)
print name_list ,"n", skill_list
```

Let's understand the program line by line. The `pickle_file = open("emp1.dat",'r')` syntax creates a file object in read mode. The `name_list = pickle.load(pickle_file)` syntax reads the first pickled object in the file and unpickles it to produce the `['mohit', 'bhaskar', 'manish']` list. Similarly, `skill_list =pickle.load(pickle_file)` reads the second pickled object in the file and unpickles it to produce the `['Python', 'Python', 'Java']` list.

Let's see the output to clear up any confusion:

Output of filepickle2.py

In `pickle,` you can not access the data randomly. `Pickle` stores and retrieves the list sequentially.

The data you dump in the `pickle` file first, would be retrieved first. This is the limitation of the `pickle` file.

Given the limitation of the `pickle` file, you can't access the list randomly, but you can use the dictionary with lists to retrieve the lists randomly.

Consider the following example:

```
leapx_team = {
name : ["mohit", "Ravender", "Himmat", "Robbin"],
skill : ["Python","Data Analytic", "Information Security", "SAP"]
        }
```

By dumping this dictionary, you can access any list randomly.

Let's see the program:

```
import pickle
pickle_file = open("emp2.dat",'w')
leapx_team = {
    'name' : ["Mohit", "Ravender", "Himmat", "Robbin"],
    'skill' : ["Python","Data Analytic", "Information Security", "SAP"]
    }
```

```
pickle.dump(leapx_team,pickle_file)
pickle_file.close()
```

In the preceding program, we have dumped a dictionary referred by name `leapx_team`. Run the preceding program and check the directory. A file named `emp2.dat` must be formed.

Let's retrieve the content of the `emp2.dat` file.

```
import pickle
pickle_file = open("emp2.dat",'r')
all_data = pickle.load(pickle_file)
print all_data["skill"]
print all_data["name"]
```

In the preceding program, `all_data` is the dictionary and we are accessing the values of the dictionary by keys.

Let's see the output:

We are accessing the list randomly.

The `pickle` module is written in Python, while the `cPickle` module is written in C language, which is faster than the `pickle` module.

Let's see the example code in `filecpickle1.py`:

```
import cPickle as pickle
name = ["mohit","bhaskar", "manish"]
skill = ["Python", "Python", "Java"]
pickle_file = open("emp1.dat","w")
pickle.dump(name,pickle_file)
pickle.dump(skill,pickle_file)
pickle_file.close()
```

Exceptions

Consider you have created a program `calc.py` and that it is running successfully. After some time, a third person edits the program `calc.py`. While executing the program, the interpreter throws some error. Due to the error, the whole program stops working. How can we avoid this situation, where, if any error occurs, then the whole program execution does not suffer?

The answer is simple: just use exception handling. Errors detected during execution are called exceptions. In the next section, you will see the example in detail, where we will see how to use exception handling with the `try...except` clause.

The try statement with an except clause

In this section, you will see how to use the `try...except` block to handle the exceptions. Let's understand the usage of the `try...except` block with examples.

Consider the following program:

```
def sum1(a,b):
        c = a+b
        return c
print sum1(10,0)
```

Consider that a third person edits the program `calc.py`; the full program is shown here:

```
def sum1(a,b):
        c = a+b
        return c
def divide(a,b):
        c = a/b
        return c
print divide(10,0)
print sum1(10,0)
```

Let's run the program:

Output of calc.py

In the preceding output, the program is showing an error because we performed division by 0. Due to one error, the whole program stop. In order to deal with the situation, we use the `try` and `except` blocks.

Let's see the program `calc.py`:

```
def sum1(a,b):
    try:
        c = a+b
        return c
    except :
        print "Error in sum1 function"
def divide(a,b):
    try:
        c = a/b
        return c
    except :
        print "Error in divide function"
print divide(10,0)
print sum1(10,0)
```

Let's run it again:

Output of calc.py

Now the `sum1()` function is giving the output `Error occurred in divide function`.

Let's discuss `try...except` in detail. First see the syntax:

```
try:
            operation block;
except Exception_name:
            If there is Exception_name1 then execute this block.
except Exception_name2:
            If there is Exception_name2, then execute this block.
  else:
            If there is no exception then execute this block.
```

In the `calc.py` program, a call to divide raises an exception; the exception is caught and the crafted message is displayed: `Error in divide function`. If no exception is raised, the program skips the except clause, continuing with the rest of the code.

Multiple exception blocks

In previous example, you learned how to catch the exceptions. But you don't know the type of error that occurred. Every exception has a certain type. The types in the example are `ZeroDivisionError`, `NameError`, and `TypeError`. Type is written in the error message. Consider a different program `divide1.py`:

```
def divide1():
    num = int(raw_input("Enter the number "))
    c = 45/num
    print c
divide1()
```

In the given program, when we give the input from the keyboard, the input string will be converted into int type.

Let's run program with different inputs:

Output of program divied.py

When we give the input 5, then the program returns 9. When we supply a string instead of a number, then the interpreter returns a message with a `ValueError` error as highlighted under red line. When number 0 is supplied, then `ZeroDivisionError` is returned. By using multiple exception blocks, you can handle both the exceptions.

Refer to the program `divide1.py`:

```
def divide1():
    try:
        num = int(raw_input("Enter the number "))
        c = 45/num
        print c
    except ValueError :
        print "Value is not int type"
    except ZeroDivisionError :
        print "Don't use zero"
    else:
        print "result is ",c
divide1()
```

In the preceding program, multiple exceptions have been handled and a crafted message has been displayed. Let's see the output:

Output of program divide1.py

In the preceding output, customized messages have been displayed so that the user can understand his mistake.

The try...finally statement

In a situation where you are completely sure that a certain block of code will be executed whether the program throws exceptions or not, `try...finally` is useful. Consider the situation when you open a file and read the input, but for some reason the program throws an exception and the file you want is closed whether the exception occurs or not, then `try...finally` will solve the problem.

The syntax is as follows:

```
try:
            #run this action first
except:
          # Run if exception occurs
Finally :
            #Always run this code
```

The order of the statement should be:

```
try -> except -> else -> finally
```

Let's discuss the code in `finally1.py`:

```
try:
    num = int(raw_input("Enter the number "))
    re = 100/num
except:
    print "Something is wrong"
else:
    print "result is ",re
finally :
    print "finally program ends"
```

In the preceding code, we used `try`, `except`, `else`, and `finally` blocks. Let's discuss the functionality by executing the code:

Output of finally1.py

In the preceding output, in the first run, `10` has been provided as the input and `try`, `else`, and `finally` blocks have been executed. In the second run, a string `Mohit` has been supplied. Due to error in type conversion `except` and `finally` blocks have been executed.

With this you have seen the importance of the `finally` statement.

The exception argument

When you write a program, it is very mundane and tedious to write each and every exception type. Instead of writing each exception, you could use just one line. See the code in `exceptiontype.py`:

```
try:
    num = int(raw_input("Enter the number "))
    re = 100/num
    print re
except Exception as e :
    print e, type(e)
```

The preceding code catches the exception as e and `type(e)` displays its exception type. Let's see the output. In the code, e is the argument of the exception: the contents referred by the argument vary by exception:

Output of program exceptiontype.py

You can see that we run the program three times. The first time we passed the value `10`. It runs successfully. In the second run, we passed string `'mohit'`, which is when the interpreter handled the exception and showed the exception message and its type. In third run, we passed 0, which is when interpreter showed the corresponding exception message and its type.

Raising exceptions

The `raise` statement allows the programmer to trigger specific exceptions explicitly.

Consider the following example:

```
>>> raise IOError
Traceback (most recent call last):
    File "<pyshell#0>", line 1, in <module>
        raise IOError
IOError
```

In the preceding example, the specific exception `IOError` has been raised by the `raise` keyword:

```
>>> raise IOError("Hi there")
Traceback (most recent call last):
 File "<pyshell#1>", line 1, in <module>
 raise IOError("Hi there")
IOError: Hi there
>>>
```

In the preceding example, a string `"Hi there"` argument has been passed, which is printed with the exception.

User-defined exceptions

In this section, we will use classes, as you have not read the Chapter 11, *Class and Objects*, you can skip the topic and get back once you complete the class and objects.

Python allows you to define your own exceptions. Exceptions should be inherited from the Exception class.

Let's discuss with an example:

```
class MyException(Exception):
    def __init__(self, value):
        self.value = value
    def __str__(self):
        return (self.value)
try:
    num = raw_input("Enter the number : ")
    if num == '2':
        raise MyException("ohh")
    else :
        print "number is not 2"
except MyException :
    print "My exception occurred"
```

Do not be afraid to see the full code.

Let's see the class part:

```
class MyException(Exception):
    def __init__(self, value):
        self.value = value
    def __str__(self):
        return (self.value)
```

The preceding code defined the MyException class, which inherits the base class Exception.

In this example, the default `__init__()` exception has been overridden.

```
try:
    num = raw_input("Enter the number : ")
    if num == '2':
        raise MyException("ohh")
```

```
         else :
               print "number is not 2"
      except MyException :
         print "My exception occurred"
```

The preceding code raises the user-defined exception if you pass the value 2. The raised exception is handled by the `except` block.

See the output of the code:

Output of code userdefined.py

In the preceding code, if you pass the value 2, then it gives a user-defined custom error. If you pass a number other than 2, then no error occurs. Let's make some changes in the code to understand the example clearly.

See the program `userdefined2.py`:

```
class MyException (Exception):
     def __init__(self, value):
         self.value = value
     def __str__(self):
         return (self.value)
try:
     num = raw_input ("Enter the number : ")
     if num == '2':
         raise MyException ("ohh")
     else :
         print "number is not 2"
except IOError:
      print "My exception occurred"
```

Just the `except` block has been changed. Now, the `except` block is only handling `IOError` not `MyException`.

Let's see the output:

Output of program userdefind2.py

When you pass a value other than 2, then the `MyException` exception is raised and the except block does not handle the raised exception. The interpreter shows the error with an exception type.

If you do not want to print an exception message, you can use pass the statement `except: pass`.

Summary

In this chapter, you learned how to read data from text files. You learned how to write data to the text files. Text files are not a good choice to store complex data such as list and dictionary. In order to store complex data, we have used `pickle` files. After that, you learned to handle exceptions. Without handling exceptions you cannot write standard code. In exceptions, you learned how to handle multiple exceptions and how to print its exception type. In end of the chapter, you learned how to create your own exception.

10
Collections

In the last chapter, we learned about functions and scope of variable. In functions, we learned about defining a function, functions with arguments, functions with arguments and return type, functions with default arguments, functions with variable length arguments, and, finally, in functions, we saw how to use key-value pairs as variable length arguments. We covered the topic of scope variable and memory management. In this chapter, we will touch the essence of every programming language, that is, collections. Some of the topics under collections such as list, dictionary, and tuple have already been covered in the previous chapter. In this chapter, we will be looking at counter, deque, ordered dictionary, default dictionary, and named tuple.

Collections

While for people with some experience in programming this is not a new topic, but those who are just taking up programming for the first time, it is a topic that will raise quite a bit of curiosity in their minds. What is a collection? The answer to this question can be well understood by the day-to-day examples from our lives. Everyone has seen a collection of stamps, collection of books, or collection of flowers, and so on. So basically we group items in a collection. What type of items does a collection contain? Pretty sure this question would be the next one. Well, a collection can contain either one type of item, for example, a collection of flowers (here, the type is flowers) or the collection can be a hybrid collection, for example, a collection of books and magazines (here, the type being books and magazines). In Python programming, each collection has unique characteristic and can be used to achieve the desired outcome. All the collections are part of the `collections` module.

More about collections can be found at the website `https://docs.python` `.org/2/library/collections.html`.

Counter

Counter is a container and it tracks the frequency of values.

 Container is a generic word, which can mean anything that can hold anything. For example, a bucket of water can be considered as container which contains water. Similarly, a list of guests can be considered as another container that holds the list.

The syntax is as follows:

```
>>>import collections
>>>collections.Counter()
```

It will be more clear with an example:

```
C:\Users\      ADMIN>python
Python 2.7.13 (v2.7.13:a06454b1afa1, Dec 17 2016, 20:42:59) [MSC v.1500 32 bit (
Intel)] on win32
Type "help", "copyright", "credits" or "license" for more information.
>>> import collections
>>> collections.Counter(['a','b','c','b','b','c','a','d','d','d','d'])
Counter({'d': 4, 'b': 3, 'a': 2, 'c': 2})
>>>
```

In the preceding screenshot, we directly use the Python command line to show the example. Before using `Counter`, you will need to import the `collections` module. In the preceding example, we pass on a list of characters to `Counter`. The `Counter` processes the list and returns the frequency of each character. Here, frequency means how many times each character occurs within the list. The outcome is in the form of dictionary, where each character of the input list becomes a key and its frequency becomes value for that key. For example, d is the key and 4 is the value which means the character d has appeared four times in the list.

Let's view another example:

```
*Python 2.7.13 Shell*
File  Edit  Shell  Debug  Options  Window  Help
Python 2.7.13 (v2.7.13:a06454b1afa1, Dec 17 2016, 20:42:59) [MSC v.1500 32
bit (Intel)] on win32
Type "copyright", "credits" or "license()" for more information.
>>> import collections
>>> collections.Counter("ONE FINE DAY")
Counter({' ': 2, 'E': 2, 'N': 2, 'A': 1, 'D': 1, 'F': 1, 'I': 1, 'O': 1, '
Y': 1})
>>>
>>>
                                                                    Ln: 7  Col: 4
```

We provide sequence of strings directly to the `Counter`. Here, in this case, even empty spaces are taken into account and their frequency is calculated:

In this example, we create a list of movies and then pass on the list to the `Counter`, which returns the frequency of the movies present in the list.

Update function

At any given time during programming, if there is a need to add more values to the existing counter, then the `update()` method can be used instead of creating a new counter. Let's look at the `update()` method of `Counter`.

```
Python 2.7.13 Shell

File  Edit  Shell  Debug  Options  Window  Help
Python 2.7.13 (v2.7.13:a06454b1afa1, Dec 17 2016, 20:42:59) [MSC v.1500 32 bit (
Intel)] on win32
Type "copyright", "credits" or "license()" for more information.
>>> import collections
>>> co=collections.Counter()
>>> co
Counter()
>>>
>>>
>>> co.update("Locarno Caine")
>>> co
Counter({'a': 2, 'o': 2, 'n': 2, ' ': 1, 'c': 1, 'e': 1, 'C': 1, 'L': 1, 'i': 1,
 'r': 1})
>>>

                                                                  Ln: 12  Col: 4
```

In the preceding example, we try to update an empty `Counter` using the `update()` method and passing `"Locarno Caine"` to the method. Thereby, the `Counter` returns frequency of each character. Did you notice that empty space also has a frequency?

```
Python 2.7.13 Shell                                                    ⬚ ▣ ✕

File  Edit  Shell  Debug  Options  Window  Help
Python 2.7.13 (v2.7.13:a06454b1afa1, Dec 17 2016, 20:42:59) [MSC v.1500 32  ▲
bit (Intel)] on win32
Type "copyright", "credits" or "license()" for more information.
>>> import collections
>>> co=collections.Counter("Lambda")
>>> co.update(" expressions")
>>> co
Counter({'s': 3, 'a': 2, 'e': 2, ' ': 1, 'b': 1, 'd': 1, 'i': 1, 'm': 1, '
L': 1, 'o': 1, 'n': 1, 'p': 1, 'r': 1, 'x': 1})
>>>
                                                                    Ln: 8  Col: 4
```

In the preceding example, we use the `update()` method to update the existing sequence of strings provided to the `Counter`.

```
Python 2.7.13 Shell                                        [_] [□] [X]

File  Edit  Shell  Debug  Options  Window  Help

Python 2.7.13 (v2.7.13:a06454b1afa1, Dec 17 2016, 20:42:59) [MSC v.15
00 32 bit (Intel)] on win32
Type "copyright", "credits" or "license()" for more information.
>>> import collections
>>> co=collections.Counter("Harry Potter")
>>> co.update({"a":2,"P":2})
>>> co
Counter({'a': 3, 'P': 3, 'r': 3, 't': 2, ' ': 1, 'e': 1, 'H': 1, 'o':
1, 'y': 1})
>>> |
                                                            Ln: 8  Col: 4
```

In the preceding case, we used the update() method to increase the frequency of
characters "a" and "P" to the existing sequence of strings. Here, we learned how
the update() method can be used to update an empty counter, update the existing input to
the counter, and increase the frequency of the existing input sequence of strings to the
counter.

Usage of counters

So far our examples were demonstrated using Python IDLE GUI. Now we will see the
usage of counter by creating a Python file. For those who did not understand what is a
Python file, read Chapter 1, *Getting Started with Python*, and then you can come back and
continue:

```
import collections

c = collections.Counter('King TutanKhamen was the youngest Pharoah')
print c
for letter in 'What a king?':
        print '%s : %d' % (letter, c[letter])
```

In the given example, we try to compare the stream of strings provided as input to the `Counter` with another stream of strings. In this case, `Counter` prints out only the frequency of the sequence of strings we want to compare and not the input string to the `Counter`:

```
C:\windows\system32\cmd.exe                                          _  □  ⌧

C:\pydev\chapter 10\code>python usage_of_counter.py
Counter({'a': 5, ' ': 5, 'h': 4, 'n': 4, 'e': 3, 't': 3, 'g': 2, 'K': 2, 'o': 2,
 's': 2, 'u': 2, 'i': 1, 'm': 1, 'P': 1, 'r': 1, 'T': 1, 'w': 1, 'y': 1})
W : 0
h : 4
a : 5
t : 3
  : 5
a : 5
  : 5
k : 0
i : 1
n : 4
g : 2
? : 0

C:\pydev\chapter 10\code>
```

Counter does not raise `KeyError` for unknown items. If a value is not found in the input string (as with `W`, `k`, and `?` in this example), then its count is `0`.

 King Tutankhamen (or Tutankhamun) ruled Egypt as pharaoh for 10 years until his death at the age of 19, around 1324 B.C. He was barely known to the modern world until 1922, when British archaeologist, Howard Carter, chiseled through a doorway and entered the boy pharaoh's tomb, which had remained sealed for more than 3,200 years. This information has been taken from `http://www.history.com/topics/ancient-history/tutank hamen`.

We will look at another example where we will deal with the basic file operations. Here, we will provide a text file, which has sentences and we will provide this file to counter as input. The following screenshot shows the text file with some texts that will serve as input to the counter:

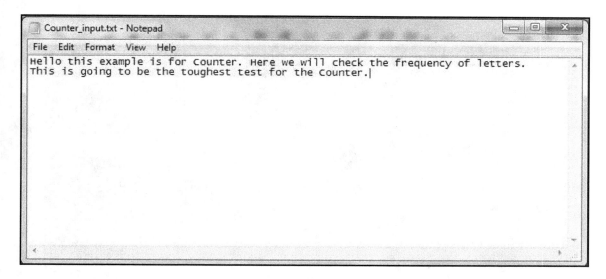

Now, let's look at the code for passing the text file as the input to the Counter:

```
import collections

co = collections.Counter()
file_txt = open("Counter_input.txt","r")
for line in file_txt:
        co.update(line.lower())
print co
```

The preceding program gives the frequency of all the characters present in the text file. We will use the `open()` function to open the file in `read` mode and `file_txt` variable serves as handle to this file handling operation. We will use the for loop and update our counter with inputs from the file one by one. The outcome is shown in the following screenshot:

There could be a scenario where you might require to choose the first five letters of higher frequency. Here you can achieve the desired outcome using the `most_common()` method.

Syntax

```
most_common(number)
```

Let's take a look at the example for the preceding scenario:

```
import collections

co = collections.Counter()
file_txt = open("Counter_input.txt","r")
for line in file_txt:
        co.update(line.lower())

print "Most common:n"
for letter, count in co.most_common(5):
        print '%s: %7d' % (letter, count)
```

We have modified our example here and now we are trying to retrieve the first 5 letters of higher frequency. Here we have simply made use of the `most_common()` method of `Counter`. The outcome is shown in the following screenshot:

```
C:\windows\system32\cmd.exe

C:\pydev\chapter 10\code>python reading_text_file1.py
Most common:
 :        24
e:        19
t:        14
h:         9
o:         9

C:\pydev\chapter 10\code>
```

Operations of Python collection counter

In Python collection counter, you can apply the sets operation such as addition, subtraction, union, and intersection. Let's take one example to illustrate the set operations:

```python
import collections

co1 = collections.Counter(['C','L','E','O','P','A','T','R','A'])
co2 = collections.Counter('JULIUS CAESAR')

print co1
print co2

print "addition n",co1 + co2 # Prints addition of sets
print "Subtractionn", co1 - co2 # Prints substration of sets

print "Union n", co1 | co2 # Prints union of sets
print "Intersection n", co1 & co2  # Prints intersection of sets
```

Here, in the preceding example, we are performing set operations on two counters. We have done addition, subtraction, union, and intersection on both the sets. The outcome is shown in the following screenshot:

```
C:\windows\system32\cmd.exe

C:\pydev\chapter 10\code>python set_operations_of_Counter.py
Counter({'A': 2, 'C': 1, 'E': 1, 'L': 1, 'O': 1, 'P': 1, 'R': 1, 'T': 1})
Counter({'A': 2, 'S': 2, 'U': 2, ' ': 1, 'C': 1, 'E': 1, 'I': 1, 'J': 1, 'L': 1,
 'R': 1})
addition
Counter({'A': 4, 'C': 2, 'E': 2, 'L': 2, 'S': 2, 'R': 2, 'U': 2, ' ': 1, 'I': 1,
 'J': 1, 'O': 1, 'P': 1, 'T': 1})
Subtraction
Counter({'P': 1, 'T': 1, 'O': 1})
Union
Counter({'A': 2, 'S': 2, 'U': 2, ' ': 1, 'C': 1, 'E': 1, 'I': 1, 'J': 1, 'L': 1,
 'O': 1, 'P': 1, 'R': 1, 'T': 1})
Intersection
Counter({'A': 2, 'C': 1, 'R': 1, 'E': 1, 'L': 1})

C:\pydev\chapter 10\code>
```

Deque

A Deque double-ended queue. It can be visualized similar to a hollow tube or pipe, which is open at the both ends. Deques allows addition and removal of elements from either ends. It will be more clear with examples:

```
import collections

de = collections.deque('India')
print 'deque:', de
print 'Lenght :', len(de)
print 'left end:', de[0]
print 'right end:', de[-1]

de.remove('a')

print 'After removing:', de
```

Here we are providing input to deque `'India'` and we are printing the left-hand side and right-hand side elements of deque using the index and then we are removing a character `'a'` from the right-hand side of the deque using `remove()`. The output will look something like this:

```
C:\windows\system32\cmd.exe                                    _ □ X

C:\pydev\chapter 10\code>python deque_example.py
deque: deque(['I', 'n', 'd', 'i', 'a'])
Lenght : 5
left end: I
right end: a
After removing: deque(['I', 'n', 'd', 'i'])

C:\pydev\chapter 10\code>
```

The `len()` function gives the length of the deque.

Populating deque

As we have already read that deque is a double-ended queue, hence it means elements can be added from either side or the deque can be populated from either side. In order to add elements or populate the deque, we have four functions: `extend()`, `append()`, `extendleft()`, and `appendleft()`. Let's take an example to illustrate how we can populate or add elements to both sides of the deque:

```
import collections
d1 = collections.deque("Google")
print d1
d1.extend('raj')
print "after extend :n", d1
d1.append('hi')
print "After append :n",d1

d1.extendleft("de")
```

```
print "after extend leftn ", d1

d1.appendleft("le")
print "after append leftn ", d1
```

Here, in this case, we are providing "Google" as input to the deque. We then extend the list by passing 'raj' as the input and it is extended to the right-hand side of the deque. We append another input to the right-hand side of the deque. In order to add elements to the left, we use extendleft() and appendleft(). The output of the program will clear the doubts as shown:

```
C:\windows\system32\cmd.exe

C:\pydev\chapter 10\code>python populating_deque.py
deque(['G', 'o', 'o', 'g', 'l', 'e'])
after extend :
deque(['G', 'o', 'o', 'g', 'l', 'e', 'r', 'a', 'j'])
After append :
deque(['G', 'o', 'o', 'g', 'l', 'e', 'r', 'a', 'j', 'hi'])
after extend left
   deque(['e', 'd', 'G', 'o', 'o', 'g', 'l', 'e', 'r', 'a', 'j', 'hi'])
after append left
   deque(['le', 'e', 'd', 'G', 'o', 'o', 'g', 'l', 'e', 'r', 'a', 'j', 'hi'])

C:\pydev\chapter 10\code>
```

 The functions extend() and append() both add elements to any collection. The only difference is that extend() adds each element to the collection one by one, while append() considers all the elements as one and appends all at the end of the collection. For example, extend(['Dunkirk','Calais']) adds two elements 'Dunkirk' and 'Calais' one by one to the collection. While append(['Dunkirk','Calais']) considers both of them as one element and adds to the end of the collection.

The extendleft() function iterates over its input and performs the equivalent of an appendleft() for each item. The final outcome is that the deque contains the input sequence in reverse order.

Deque consumption

Deque can be consumed from either both ends or one end. For consuming deque elements or retrieval of elements, we use two functions: `pop()` and `popleft()`. It will be more clear with an example:

```python
import collections
d1 = collections.deque("abcdefghacmqdcb")
print d1
print "Poped element ",d1.pop()
print d1
print "Poped left element ",d1.popleft()
print d1
```

Here we use `pop` to remove the elements one at a time from right end of the deque. In this case, char b is removed from the right end of the deque. The `popleft()` function removes element from the left end of the deque. Here, `popleft()` removed char a from the left end of the deque as shown:

```
C:\pydev\chapter 10\code>python deque_consumption.py
deque(['a', 'b', 'c', 'd', 'e', 'f', 'g', 'h', 'a', 'c', 'm', 'q', 'd', 'c', 'b'
])
Poped element  b
deque(['a', 'b', 'c', 'd', 'e', 'f', 'g', 'h', 'a', 'c', 'm', 'q', 'd', 'c'])
Poped left element  a
deque(['b', 'c', 'd', 'e', 'f', 'g', 'h', 'a', 'c', 'm', 'q', 'd', 'c'])

C:\pydev\chapter 10\code>
```

Deque rotation

Deque rotation allows rotation of items on either side. For right-side rotation, the notation is (+n) and for left-side rotation, the notation used is (-n), where n is the number of rotations:

```
import collections

d = collections.deque(xrange(6))
print "Normal queue", d

d.rotate(2)
print "nRight rotation :", d

d1 = collections.deque(xrange(6))
d1.rotate(-2)
print "nleft rotation :", d1
```

In this case, using the xrange() function we generate a list of 5 numbers, which will serve as input to our deque. We rotate the deque on the right side and then on the left side. The results can be seen here:

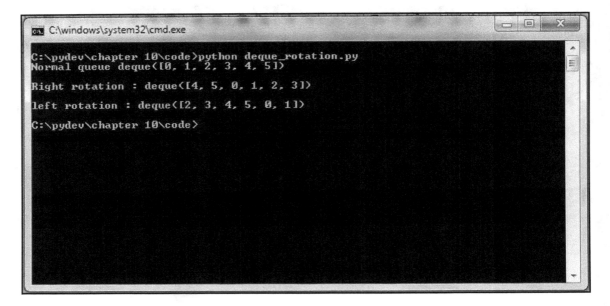

From the output, we can observe that in the right rotation, items are shifted to the right direction. In the left rotation, the items are shifted to the left direction.

Ordered dictionary

The OrderedDict is a subclass of the dictionary and it remembers the order in which the elements are added:

Syntax

```
d1 = collections.OrderedDict()
d1 is ordered dictionary here.
```

Let's look at the comparison between dictionary and ordered dictionary:

```
import collections
print 'Regular Dictionary'
d = {}
d['a']= 'SAS'
d['b']= 'PYTHON'
d['c']= 'R'

for k,v in d.items():
        print k, ":",v

print 'n Ordered dictionary'

d1 = collections.OrderedDict()
d1['a']= 'SAS'
d1['b']= 'PYTHON'
d1['c']= 'R'

for k,v in d1.items():
        print k, ":",v
```

Here, we create a normal dictionary and an ordered dictionary. Both the outputs are shown here:

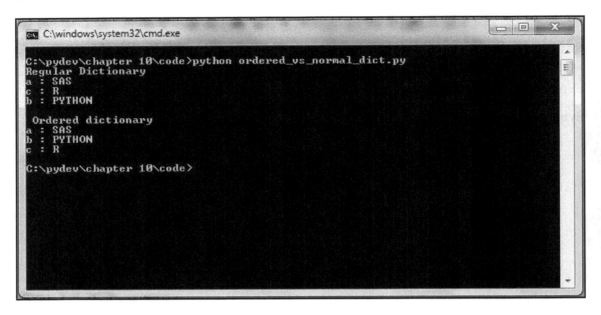

As we could see, the ordered dictionary has retained the order in which the elements were added.

Sorting of ordered dictionary based upon keys

We can sort the ordered dictionary using the `sorted()` function:

Syntax

```
dict = collections.OrderedDict(sorted(d1.items()))
dict = New sorted dictionary
d1= Original Order dictionary
```

Let's take an example to understand the `sorted()` function. For a refresher on `sorted()` function, you can revisit Chapter 4, *Lists*:

```
import collections
print 'n Order dictionary'
d1 = collections.OrderedDict()
d1['a']= 'SAS'
d1['d']= 'PYTHON'
```

```
d1['b']= 'JULIA'
d1['f']= 'R'
d1['c']= 'SPARK'

for k,v in d1.items():
        print k, ":",v
print 'n Sorted Order dictionary'
dict = collections.OrderedDict(sorted(d1.items()))

for k,v in dict.items():
        print k, ":",v
```

Here we create an ordered dictionary d1 and then sort it using the `sorted()` function. The following output will make it more clear:

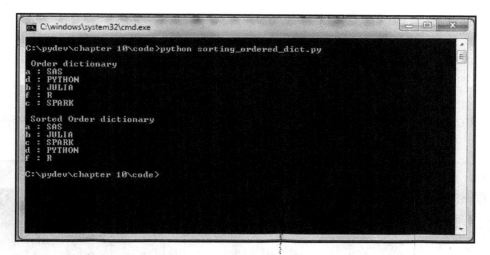

By default, the dictionary is sorted according to keys.

Sorting of ordered dictionary based upon values

We can also sort the ordered dictionary based upon values:

Syntax

```
dict = collections.OrderedDict(sorted(d1.items(), key=lambda (k,v): v))
dict = New sorted dictionary
d1= Original Ordered dictionary
```

Here, the lambda function changes the key to its value. As ordered, the dictionary returns the `(key, value)` pair. The lambda function makes `key = value`, thus the ordered dictionary will be sorted by its value. Let's take an example to understand the sorting of the ordered dictionary based upon values:

```
import collections
print 'n Order dictionary'
d1 = collections.OrderedDict()
d1['a']= 'SAS'
d1['d']= 'PYTHON'
d1['b']= 'SAP HANNA'
d1['f']= 'R'
d1['c']= 'JULIA'

for k,v in d1.items():
        print k, ":",v
print 'n Sorted Order dictionary'
dict = collections.OrderedDict(sorted(d1.items(), key=lambda (k,v): v))

for k,v in dict.items():
        print k, ":",v
```

As you can clearly see from the preceding example, the `lambda()` function converts `key` to `value` and we can see the output as shown here:

```
C:\windows\system32\cmd.exe

C:\pydev\chapter 10\code>python sorting_ordered_dict_based_on_values.py
 Order dictionary
a : SAS
d : PYTHON
b : SAP HANNA
f : R
c : JULIA
 Sorted Order dictionary
c : JULIA
d : PYTHON
f : R
b : SAP HANNA
a : SAS

C:\pydev\chapter 10\code>
```

The lambda function is explained in the special function section.

Default dictionary

So far we have learned about regular dictionary and ordered dictionary. In this section, we will learn a special type of dictionary called default dictionary, which is provided by the `defaultdict` module of collections. A `defaultdict` works exactly the way a normal `dict` does, but it is initialized with a callable function called `default_factory()` that takes no arguments and provides a default value for a nonexistent key.

Syntax

```
defaultdict(default_factory())
```

We will try to understand with two examples:

```
from collections import defaultdict

def func():
        return "Cricket"

game = defaultdict(func)

game["A"]= "Football"
game["B"] = "Badminton"

print game
print game["A"]
print game["B"]
print game["C"]
```

In this case, our function or function `func` acts as a `default_factory` function. We have assigned `game["A"]= "Football"`, where `"A"` is the key. If key is new (not found in the dictionary `"game"`), then `defaultdict` does not give an error; instead, it returns the default value, which is returned by the `default_factory()` function. So, for the new key `"C"`, the default value is `"Cricket"`.

This will be more clear with the mentioned output:

```
C:\windows\system32\cmd.exe

C:\pydev\chapter 10\code>python default_dict_example.py
defaultdict(<function func at 0x022F8D70>, {'A': 'Football', 'B': 'Badminton'}>
Football
Badminton
Cricket

C:\pydev\chapter 10\code>
```

The preceding task can be achieved by following the lambda function. Let's understand with an example:

```
from collections import defaultdict
game = defaultdict(lambda : "Cricket")

game["A"]= "Football"
game["B"] = "Badminton"

print game
print game["A"]
print game["B"]
print game["C"]
```

Here, we just used the lambda function, which initializes the default value of `"Cricket"` if any new key is encountered:

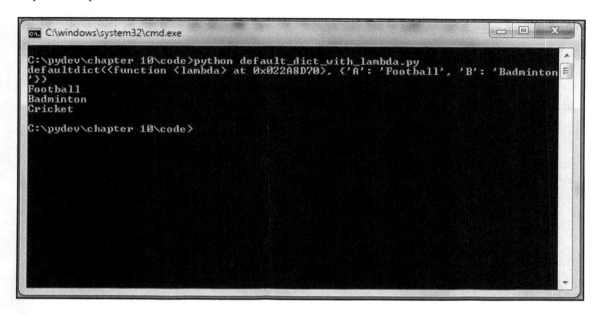

Now, next we will use int as `default_factory` function. The default value for int is 0:

```
from collections import defaultdict

game = defaultdict(int)

game["A"]= "Football"
game["B"] = "Badminton"

print game
print game["A"]
print game["B"]
print game["C"]
```

Here, we just initialized the int value for any new key encountered. For game ["C"], the output returned is 0:

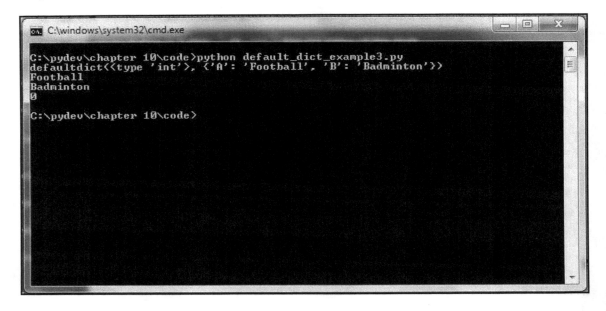

Sample problem solved by the default dictionary - scenario one

Let's consider a simple problem solved by default dictionary; here we would like to calculate the frequency of elements present in the list. Let's examine the scenario with an example:

```
from collections import defaultdict

game = defaultdict(int)

list1 = ['cricket', 'badminton', 'hockey' 'rugby', 'golf', 'baseball' ,
'football']

for each in list1:
        game[each]= game[each]+1

print game
```

As the default value is initialized with 0 we have incremented it with 1, and, in this way, we can calculate the frequency of elements present in the list:

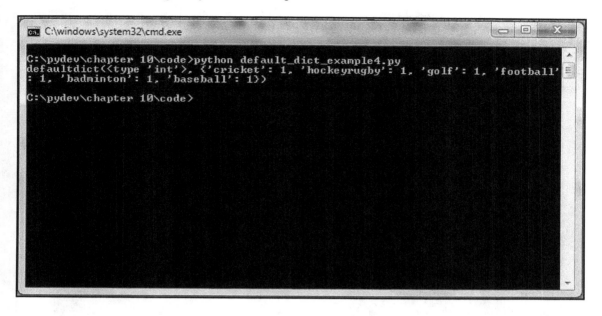

Sample problem solved by the default dictionary - scenario two

Let's analyze a scenario where we have a list of tuple pairs. The list `tuple_list_county = [('US', 'Visconsin'), ('Germany', 'Bavaria'), ('UK', 'Bradfordshire'), ('India', 'punjab'), ('China', 'Shandong'), ('Canada', 'Nova Scotia')]` is the pair of `(Country, county)`. So our aim is to make our county or state as `key` and `country` as the list of values. Let's do it with the following code:

```
from collections import defaultdict

game = defaultdict(list)

tuple_list_county =  [('US', 'Visconsin'), ('Germany', 'Bavaria'), ('UK',
'Bradfordshire'), ('India', 'punjab'), ('China', 'Shandong'), ('Canada',
'Nova Scotia')]

print game["any_value"]

for k,v in tuple_list_county:
```

```
    game[k].append(v)

print game
```

Here, the default value is the list itself. The first value of the tuple is fixed as key and the second value is appended:

```
C:\windows\system32\cmd.exe                                    —  □  ☒

C:\pydev\chapter 10\code>python default_dict_list_of_tuples.py
[]
defaultdict(<type 'list'>, {'Canada': ['Nova Scotia'], 'any_value': [], 'India':
['punjab'], 'US': ['Visconsin'], 'China': ['Shandong'], 'UK': ['Bradfordshire']
, 'Germany': ['Bavaria']})

C:\pydev\chapter 10\code>
```

Named tuple

Python facilitates you to create your own data type. In the Python collection, namedtuple gives you a special feature to create your own data type. In the C language, you might have used struct to create your own data type. When you want to create a new data type, you would like to explore the answers to some questions as what should be the name of the new data type? What are the fields of the new data type? Let's discuss this with a syntax and an example of namedtuple.

Syntax

```
collections.namedtuple(typename, field_names[, verbose=False][,
rename=False])
```

Let's try to understand the syntax of `namedtuple`. In the preceding syntax:

- The `typename` defines the name of the new data type
- The `field_names` can be a sequence of strings such as `['x', 'y']` or string in which values are whitespaced or , separated
- If verbose is `False`, then the class definition would not be printed, it is a good idea to keep it `False`
- If rename is `False`, then the invalid field names are automatically replaced with positional names, for example, `'def, age, empid'` is converted to `'_0 , age, empid'` because `def` is a keyword

Let's discuss with an example:

```
import collections
employee = collections.namedtuple('emp','name, age, empid')

record1 = employee("Hamilton", 28, 12365 )

print "Record is ", record1
print "name of employee is ", record1.name
print "age of employee is ", record1.empid

print "type is ",type(record1)
```

Here, we create a `namedtuple` emp, which will contain the name of the employee, his/her age and the employee ID. We print out the complete record along with `name`, `empid`, and what type of record `namedtuple` contains. In order to access the values of `namedtuple`, we use the `.` operator along with the name of the tuple. As the `namedtuple` contains the record type as `emp`, the outcome displays the same as shown here:

```
C:\windows\system32\cmd.exe

C:\pydev\chapter 10\code>python named_tuple.py
Record is   emp<name='Hamilton', age=28, empid=12365>
name of employee is   Hamilton
age of employee is   12365
type is  <class '__main__.emp'>

C:\pydev\chapter 10\code>
```

Adding values and creating a dictionary

In the next example, we will understand how to add list values into `namedtuple` and how to make dictionary from `namedtuple`:

```python
import collections
employee = collections.namedtuple('emp','name, age, empid')
list1 = ['BOB', 21, 34567]
record2 =employee._make(list1)
print record2
print "n"
print (record2._asdict())
```

Here, by using `_make`, we can add a list into a `namedtuple` and by using `_asdict` we can create dictionary of `namedtuple`:

```
C:\windows\system32\cmd.exe

C:\pydev\chapter 10\code>python named_tuple_with_list_values.py
emp(name='BOB', age=21, empid=34567)

OrderedDict([('name', 'BOB'), ('age', 21), ('empid', 34567)])

C:\pydev\chapter 10\code>
```

Now, consider a scenario where you would like to replace a value from `namedtuple`. Like tuple, the `namedtuple` is also immutable. But you can use the `_replace` function to replace the value from `namedtuple`:

```
import collections
employee = collections.namedtuple('emp','name, age, empid')

record1 = employee("Marina", 28, 12365 )

print "Record is ", record1
print "n"
print  record1._replace(age= 25)
print "n"
print "Record is ", record1
print "n"
record1 = record1._replace(age= 25)
print "Record is ", record1
```

Here, we are simply using the dot (.) operator followed by the _replace() function and providing the new value as an input to the _replace() function. In this way, we can replace the existing value in a namedtuple:

```
C:\windows\system32\cmd.exe

C:\pydev\chapter 10\code>python replacing_value_from_named_tuple.py
Record is  emp(name='Marina', age=28, empid=12365)

emp(name='Marina', age=25, empid=12365)

Record is  emp(name='Marina', age=28, empid=12365)

Record is  emp(name='Marina', age=25, empid=12365)
C:\pydev\chapter 10\code>
```

Summary

In collections, we learned about collections, and asked what are collections? What is their importance in any programming language? We learned about different types of collections, which are available in the Python programming language. We learned about module collection and its various members, which we import in our code. We also learned about counter, deque, ordered dictonary, default dictionary, and finally namedtuple. In the next chapter, we will take some object-oriented programming (OOPs) concepts and we will see how Python supports the OOPs concepts.

11
Class and Objects

Before we delve deeper into classes and objects, let's first try to understand what they are and why they form part of Python programming. Python language also supports object-oriented programming. For beginners, this might be a little confusing topic but be assured it is not that difficult to understand the concept of object-oriented programming (OOP). Let's try to understand what object-oriented programming is. Before this concept was introduced, we were primarily slave to writing procedural programming, that is, going line by line. At this level, you need not understand what is procedural programming but certainly there is one example to illustrate it, that is, C language. In procedural programming, there were a lot of complexities and above all procedural programming had negligible code reuse concept.

Object-oriented programming overview

The concept of object-oriented programming was seen to solve many problems, which procedural programming did not solve. In object-oriented programming, everything mimics just like a real-world object. In the real world, everything is an object. An object can have state and behavior. An object in the real world can communicate with another object. For example, a dog object in the real world has state and behavior. OOPs is based on four pillars. They are:

- Polymorphism
- Inheritance
- Abstraction
- Encapsulation

Key concepts

OOPs is a vast topic that needs to be covered at the intermediate level. In case of Python programming, however, we will cover some key concepts in this chapter.

- **Class**: Class is considered as a blueprint for object creation. It can be understood as a factory to produce objects. It provides a template for creating an object and specifying its behavior through means of methods and state through means of variable instance name.
- **Objects**: They can be considered as an instance of a class. An object can have state and behavior or attributes. The objects basically bundles a set of related states and behaviors, for example, a dog has state (*name*) and behavior (*barking*).
- **Inheritance**: Inheritance is a feature supported by many programming languages, it can be correlated in real life as properties passed on by parents to their children. In object-oriented programming, the child class can inherit many properties from the parent class. Here, we mean that the child class can use an existing method or behavior, which the parent class has defined and use them accordingly in their class. Inheritance can be a single inheritance or multiple inheritance. Single inheritance, as the name suggests, refers to only one parent, while multiple inheritance refers to inheriting the property from multiple parents.
- **Polymorphism**: Well, this literally means something, which has many forms. In OOPs, an object can have many forms through means of different attributes. To simplify, in our case, we can understand it by methods with the same name but having different outputs.
- **Abstraction**: Here, we hide the necessary details and are only interested in showing the relevant details to the other intended user. Here, by other intended user we mean another software application, or another class, or other client who will be the end users of the program.
- **Encapsulation**: This refers to hiding the necessary methods and their relevant details from the outside world. A class can be treated as a best example, which provides encapsulation to the methods and relevant instances.

Creating a class

Now, after understanding some basic concepts of OOPs, let's understand them with some programming.

Creating a class in Python is quite easy. Refer to the following syntax:

```
class <class name >(<parent class name>):
     <method definition-1>
     <method definition-n>
```

Let's create a `class1.py` program. In this program, we are creating an empty class:

```
class Leapx_org():
 pass
```

We have just created a `Leapx_org` class. This class is empty, the class body just contains the pass statement. Basically, the class is a blueprint to create instances. Let's create the instances:

```
L_obj1 = Leapx_org()
L_obj2 = Leapx_org()
print L_obj1
print L_obj2
```

Let's run the `class1.py` program:

Output of program class1.py

In the preceding screenshot, you can see both the instances of the `Leapx_org` class at different locations in memory.

Instance variables

Instance variables refer to the data that are unique to instances (objects). Let's create an instance variable. We will write a new `class2.py` program:

```
class Leapx_org():
 pass
```

```
L_obj1 = Leapx_org()
L_obj2 = Leapx_org()
L_obj1.f_name = "Mohit"
L_obj1.L_name = "RAJ"
L_obj1.pamount = "60000"
L_obj2.f_name = "Ravender"
L_obj2.L_name = "Dahiya"
L_obj2.pamount = "70000"
print L_obj1.f_name+ " "+ L_obj1.L_name
print L_obj2.f_name+ " "+ L_obj2.L_name
```

In the preceding code, L_obj1.f_name, L_obj1.L_name, and L_obj1.pamount are the instance variables, which are unique to the L_obj1 instance. Similarly, L_obj2.f_name, L_obj2.L_name, and L_obj2.pamount are the instance variables of the L_obj2 instance.

Let's run the code:

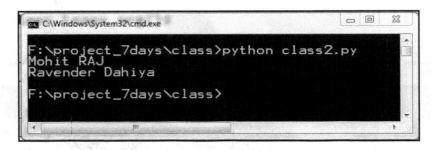

Output of code class2.py

If we create an instance variable, as shown in the code, then we would not get benefit of making a class. You can see repeatable code for both the instances. So we would not have to set the variable all the time. In order to make it automatically, we will use the special method __init__() function.

The __init__ method

The __init__() method must begin and end with two consecutive underscores. Here __init__ works as the class's constructor. When a user instantiates the class, it runs automatically.

Let's see and understand this concept with the help of code. Here we will write the full code for `classinit.py` and then we will understand it line by line:

```
class Leapx_org():
   def __init__(self,first,last,pay):
      self.f_name = first
      self.l_name = last
      self.pay_amt = pay
      self.full_name = first+" "+last
L_obj1 = Leapx_org('mohit', 'RAJ', 60000)
L_obj2 = Leapx_org('Ravender', 'Dahiya',70000)
print L_obj1.full_name
print L_obj2.full_name
```

So, from preceding code, it seems difficult; let's understand it by line by line. The first line defines a class as we already know. When we create the `__init__(self,first,last,pay)` method inside the class then first argument, self, of `__init__()` method receives the instance of the class automatically. By convention we call it `self`, you can use another name, but it is a good idea to stick to the convention. After declaring the `self` variable, we can specify other arguments that we want to accept. So we will accept three values `first`, `last`, and `pay`. Inside the `__init__()` method we will declare the instance variable. So the `self.f_name`, `self.l_name`, `self.pay_amt`, and `self.full_name` are instance variables. The `self` variable receives the instance. The `self.f_name = first` statement is the same thing as we saw `L_obj1.f_name = "Mohit"` in the previous code `class2.py`. The `L_obj` is the instance of the class and the variable is self referred to instance of the class, which is more or less similar. When we create an instance like `L_obj1 = Leapx_org('mohit', 'RAJ', 60000)` the values `('mohit', 'RAJ', 60000)` are automatically passed to the `__init__(self, first, last, pay)` method. We don't need to pass the value of the `self` variable, because the `L_obj1` instance is passed automatically.

Similar things happens for the L_obj2 instance. If your doubt still persists for the self and instance variables, you can refer to the following figure for clarification:

```
1   class Leapx_org():
2       def __init__(self,first,last,pay):
3           self.f_name = first
4           self.l_name = last
5           self.pay_amt = pay
6           self.full_name = first+" "+last
7
8
9   L_obj1 = Leapx_org('mohit', 'RAJ', 60000)
10  L_obj2 = Leapx_org('Ravender', 'Dahiya',70000)
11
12  print L_obj1.full_name
13  print L_obj2.full_name
```

Self linking with object

Now you got an idea of the instance variable: the self.f_name, self.l_name, self_pay_amt, and self.full_name are the instance variables, unique to instance L_obj1 and L_obj2. The self.f_name, self.l_name, self_pay_amt, and self.full_name contain values mohit, RAJ, and 60000, for instance, L_obj1 and Ravender, Dahiya and 70000, for instance, L_obj2, respectively.

Let's run the code:

```
C:\Windows\System32\cmd.exe

F:\project_7days\class>python classinit.py
mohit RAJ
Ravender Dahiya

F:\project_7days\class>
```

Output of classinit.py

You can see that the preceding result and the result from class2.py are the same. But we reduce few lines from the code classinit.py.

Let's create the method inside the class. We want a functionality to generate the e-mail address for users. We will write the full code for `classmethod1.py` and discuss it:

```
class Leapx_org():
  def __init__(self,first,last,pay):
    self.f_name = first
    self.l_name = last
    self.pay_amt = pay
    self.full_name = first+" "+last
  def make_email(self):
    return self.f_name+ "."+self.l_name+"@xyz.com"
L_obj1 = Leapx_org('mohit', 'RAJ', 60000)
L_obj2 = Leapx_org('Ravender', 'Dahiya',70000)
print L_obj1.full_name
print L_obj1.make_email()
print L_obj2.full_name
print L_obj2.make_email()
```

The code is very much similar to the previous code. We added the `make_email()` method here, which used the instance variables `self.f_name` and `self.l_name`. By using the `L_obj1.make_email()` syntax the `L_obj1` instance calls the `method` `make_email()` method.

The `make_email()` is the regular method. What is the regular method? The regular methods in the class automatically take the instances as the first argument. That's why, by convention, we use self as the first argument which expects an instance.

If you remember, in string, list we did the same thing as we did in `list1.append()`. If you relate list with the preceding class, then `list1` is the instance and `append()` is the method of the class list. You can also define the list as shown here:

```
List1 = list()
```

Let's go deeper to explore the `self` variable. If you are still in doubt, the next example will clear it. Refer to the code in `classmethod2.py` as follows:

```
class Leapx_org():
  def __init__(self,first,last,pay):
    self.f_name = first
    self.l_name = last
    self.pay_amt = pay
    self.full_name = first+" "+last
  def make_email():
    return self.f_name+ "."+self.l_name+"@xyz.com"
L_obj1 = Leapx_org('mohit', 'RAJ', 60000)
print L_obj1.make_email()
```

The preceding code is very much similar to `classmethod2.py`. In order to experiment, we used just one instance `L_obj1`. In the `make_email()` method, the argument self has been removed. Let's run the code:

Output of code classmethod2.py

You can see that error `make_email() takes no arguments (1 given)`. This can be confusing as we have not passed any argument in the syntax `L_obj1.make_email()`. What is the `make_email()` method expecting? In this case, the `L_obj1` instance is passed automatically. That's why we use the `self` argument to the methods of the class.

Let's see following code `classmethod3.py` in order to understand this better:

```
class Leapx_org():
  def __init__(self,first,last,pay):
    self.f_name = first
    self.l_name = last
    self.pay_amt = pay
    self.full_name = first+" "+last
  def make_email(self):
    return self.f_name+ "."+self.l_name+"@xyz.com"
L_obj1 = Leapx_org('mohit', 'RAJ', 60000)
print L_obj1.make_email()
print Leapx_org.make_email(L_obj1)
```

In the preceding code, the `self` variable has been put in the `make_email(self)` method. In the last line, `Leapx_org.make_email(L_obj1)` signifies what is running in the background. The syntax `L_obj1.make_email()` and `Leapx_org.make_email(L_obj1)` both are one and the same.

The syntax `Leapx_org.make_email(L_obj1)` states `class.method(instance)`. In this syntax, we pass the instance to the `make_email()` method and the `self` argument accepts that instance. So, `L_obj1.make_email()` is transformed into `Leapx_org.make_email(L_obj1)`.

Class variables

Class variables are the ones, which are sharable among all the instances of the class. The class variable must be the same for all the instances. To understand with example, let's assume that `leapx_org` gives 5 percent increment based upon `pay_amt`. Let's use another method to calculate the increment. Refer to the `classinstance1.py` program:

```
class Leapx_org():
  def __init__(self,first,last,pay):
    self.f_name = first
    self.l_name = last
    self.pay_amt = pay
    self.full_name = first+" "+last
  def make_email(self):
    return self.f_name+ "."+self.l_name+"@xyz.com"
  def incrementpay(self):
    self.pay_amt = int(self.pay_amt*1.20)
    return self.pay_amt
L_obj1 = Leapx_org('mohit', 'RAJ', 60000)
L_obj2 = Leapx_org('Ravender', 'Dahiya',70000)
print L_obj1.pay_amt
print L_obj1.incrementpay()
```

There are a couple of things that are new in the preceding program. We added `incrementpay()` which returns the raised `pay_amt` amount. The last line `print L_obj1.incrementpay()` states that the `L_obj1` instance calls the `incrementpay()` method. Let's run the program:

Output of classinstance1.py

The preceding program runs successfully but most of its content is logically wrong. In the `incrementpay()` method, we used the multiplication number `1.20`, which would be same for all the instances. So we can make the multiplication number `1.20` as the class variable.

Let's write the new code `classinstance2.py` with amendments:

```
class Leapx_org():
    mul_num = 1.20
    def __init__(self,first,last,pay):
        self.f_name = first
        self.l_name = last
        self.pay_amt = pay
        self.full_name = first+" "+last
    def make_email(self):
        return self.f_name+ "."+self.l_name+"@xyz.com"
    def incrementpay(self):
        self.pay_amt = int(self.pay_amt*self.mul_num)
        return self.pay_amt
L_obj1 = Leapx_org('mohit', 'RAJ', 60000)
L_obj2 = Leapx_org('Ravender', 'Dahiya',70000)
print L_obj1.pay_amt
print L_obj1.incrementpay()
```

In the preceding program, we made a `mul_num` class variable that contains the value `1.20`. In the `incrementpay()` method, we access the `mul_num` class variable with the help of `self` means instance. You can use either `self` or class name with the `mul_num`. If you use the class name with `mul_num`, then it would be `Leapx_org. mul_num`. If you don't use any of them, then the interpreter throws an error. You might be confused, if it is a class variable, then how can we access the class variable with the instance. Let's add some lines to understand it better. Add the following lines at the end of the code:

```
print L_obj1.mul_num
print L_obj2.mul_num
print Leapx_org.mul_num
```

Run the program and see the output:

Output of program classinstance2 with added lines

As you can see, we are accessing the `mul_num` class variable with the help of instances `L_obj1`, `L_obj2`, and the `Leapx_org` class. All are showing the same value `1.2`. So what happens when we try to access an attribute by an instance? The instance first checks whether the instance contains the attribute. If the instance does not contain the attribute, then it checks the class or its parent class contains that attribute. So the instances `L_obj1` and `L_obj2` access the `mul_num` from the class. For more clarification, you can view the attribute of the class and instances.

The following is the full code of `classinstance3.py`:

```python
class Leapx_org():
    mul_num = 1.20
    def __init__(self,first,last,pay):
        self.f_name = first
        self.l_name = last
        self.pay_amt = pay
        self.full_name = first+" "+last

    def make_email(self):
        return self.f_name+ "."+self.l_name+"@xyz.com"

    def incrementpay(self):
        self.pay_amt = int(self.pay_amt*self.mul_num)
        return self.pay_amt

L_obj1 = Leapx_org('mohit', 'RAJ', 60000)
L_obj2 = Leapx_org('Ravender', 'Dahiya',70000)
print "instance space ",L_obj1.__dict__
print "class space ",Leapx_org.__dict__
```

Except for the last two lines, the rest of the code is similar to the previous one. The `L_obj1.__dict__` syntax prints all the attributes of the `L_obj1` instance and `Leapx_org.__dict__` prints all the attributes of the `Leapx_org` class. Run the program to see the output:

Output of code classinstance3.py

You can see that the instance name space does not contain the `mul_num` class variable, but the class name space contains `mul_num`. Let's add `mul_num` to the name space of the `L_obj1` instance. To avoid confusion, we will write `classinstance4.py`:

```python
class Leapx_org():
    mul_num = 1.20
    def __init__(self,first,last,pay):
        self.f_name = first
        self.l_name = last
        self.pay_amt = pay
        self.full_name = first+" "+last

    def make_email(self):
        return self.f_name+ "."+self.l_name+"@xyz.com"

    def incrementpay(self):
        self.pay_amt = int(self.pay_amt*self.mul_num)
        return self.pay_amt

L_obj1 = Leapx_org('mohit', 'RAJ', 60000)
L_obj2 = Leapx_org('Ravender', 'Dahiya',70000)
L_obj1.mul_num = 1.3

print "instance space L_obj1 n",L_obj1.__dict__
print "ninstance space L_obj2 n",L_obj2.__dict__
print "nclass space n",Leapx_org.__dict__

print L_obj1.mul_num
print L_obj2.mul_num
print Leapx_org.mul_num
```

In the preceding code, line `L_obj1.mul_num = 1.3` adds the `mul_num` variable in the name space of the `L_obj1` instance. The last three lines of code print the name of space of the instance `L_obj1`, `L_obj2` and the `Leapx_org` class. Let's run the code:

Output of code classinstance4.py

The preceding output shows that the `L_obj1` instance finds the `mul_num` first with its own namespace before searching in the class namespace. That's why `L_obj1` shows 1.3. We did not set `mul_num`, for instance, `L_obj2`, so `L_obj2` is still getting the value from the class namespace. In the `incrementpay()` method, we use `self.mul_num` instead of `Leapx_org.mul_num` because `self.mul_num` gives the ability to change `mul_num` value for single instance, if we want to. Let's create one more class variable to count the number of employees.

Let us see the next code `classinstance5.py`:

```python
class Leapx_org():
    mul_num = 1.20
    count= 0
    def __init__(self,first,last,pay):
        self.f_name = first
        self.l_name = last
        self.pay_amt = pay
        self.full_name = first+" "+last
        Leapx_org.count = Leapx_org.count+1

    def make_email(self):
        return self.f_name+ "."+self.l_name+"@xyz.com"

    def incrementpay(self):
        self.pay_amt = int(self.pay_amt*self.mul_num)
        return self.pay_amt
```

```
L_obj1 = Leapx_org('mohit', 'RAJ', 60000)
L_obj2 = Leapx_org('Ravender', 'Dahiya',70000)
L_obj3 = Leapx_org('Bhaskar', 'DAS',70000)
print "Number of Employees are : ", Leapx_org.count
```

Earlier we created new class variables count initializing with 0. The syntax
`Leapx_org.count = Leapx_org.count+1` increases the class variable by one. We have
created three instances. Whenever we create a new instance, the `count` variable is
incremented by one. Let's see the output:

Output of code classinstance5.py

Now you got the idea of the class variable. If you set `self.count = self.count+1`
instead of `Leapx_org.count = Leapx_org.count+1`, then you would get 0 employees.

Class inheritance

In this section, we will learn about inheritance. Inheritance allows us to inherit methods and
attributes of the parent class. By inheritance, a new child class automatically gets all of the
methods and attributes of the existing parent class. The syntax is given as follows:

```
class DerivedClassName(BaseClassName):
   <statement-1>
   .
   . .
   <statement-N>
```

If you remember, in `Chapter 10`, *File Handling and Exceptions*, we had inherited the built-in
class exception. Starting with the existing code, let's make the `instructor` class, which
would inherit the method of the `Leapx_org` class. Refer to the code in `classinheri1.py`:

```
class Leapx_org():
   mul_num = 1.20
   count= 0
   def __init__(self,first,last,pay):
```

```
        self.f_name = first
        self.l_name = last
        self.pay_amt = pay
        self.full_name = first+" "+last
        Leapx_org.count = Leapx_org.count+1

    def make_email(self):
        return self.f_name+ "."+self.l_name+"@xyz.com"

    def incrementpay(self):
        self.pay_amt = int(self.pay_amt*self.mul_num)
        return self.pay_amt

class instructor(Leapx_org):
    pass
I_obj1 = instructor('mohit', 'RAJ', 60000)
I_obj2 = instructor('Ravender', 'Dahiya',70000)
print "number of employees ", instructor.count
print I_obj1.make_email()
print I_obj2.make_email()
```

In preceding code, we create a new class instructor which inherits the method and attributes from the `Leapx_org` class. The `Leapx_org` class is the base class and the instructor class is the child class. We left the body of the instructor class blank. We created two instances of the instructor class, then we printed the e-mails. Let's run the code:

Output of code classinheri1.py

The preceding result shows that the child class is successfully accessing the attributes of the parent class. When we instantiate the instructor class, it first looks up the __init__ method of the instructor class. As the instructor class is empty, the interpreter checks the chain of inheritance. If you want to check the chain of inheritance, you need to use the `help()` function.

Add the following lines in the `classinheri1.py` code and run it:

Output of the help function

In the preceding screenshot, you can easily see which methods, data, and attributes inherit from the base class. You can say that the base class is generic class and the child class is a specific class. Let's proceed to more complicated examples. In the instructor class, we will add one more thing, which instructor teaches which subject. In order to do that, we need to add the `__init__` method to the instructor class. Let's see the code `classinheri2.py` and discuss the additions:

```python
class Leapx_org():
    mul_num = 1.20
    count= 0
    def __init__(self,first,last,pay):
        self.f_name = first
        self.l_name = last
        self.pay_amt = pay
        self.full_name = first+" "+last
        Leapx_org.count = Leapx_org.count+1

    def make_email(self):
        return self.f_name+ "."+self.l_name+"@xyz.com"

    def incrementpay(self):
```

```
        self.pay_amt = int(self.pay_amt*self.mul_num)
        return self.pay_amt

class instructor(Leapx_org):
    def __init__(self,first,last,pay, subject):
    Leapx_org.__init__(self,first,last,pay)
    self.subject = subject

I_obj1 = instructor('mohit', 'RAJ', 60000, "Python")
I_obj2 = instructor('Ravender', 'Dahiya',70000, "Data Analytic")
print I_obj1.make_email()
print I_obj1.subject
print I_obj2.make_email()
print I_obj2.subject
```

In the class instructor, we have created a new __init__ method, which accepts the data first, last, pay, and subject. Now, there is no need to copy and paste the code of the __init__ method from the Leapx_org base class. In order to get the data of the first, last, and pay arguments, we have used the Leapx_org.__init__(self,first,last,pay) syntax. This syntax passes the first, last, and pay arguments to the Leapx_org base class. The arguments first, last, and pay are handled by the Leapx_org class and the subject argument is handled by the class instructor.

We created two instances I_obj1 and l_obj2, which pass the data to the instructor class. Let's run the code:

Output of code classinheri2.py

Now you can understand that by using this class we can avoid repeating a lot of code.

Multiple inheritance

In multiple inheritance, a class inherits the attributes and methods from more than one parent class. Let's take a simple example `classmultiple.py`:

```
class A():
    def sum1(self,a,b):
      c = a+b
      return c
class B():
    def sub1(self,a,b):
      c = a-b
      return c
class C(A,B):
    pass
c_obj = C()
print "Sum is ", c_obj.sum1(12,4)
print "After substraction ",c_obj.sub1(45,5)
```

In the preceding code, we have created three classes. Class A contains a `sum1()` method, which performs the sum of two numbers. Class B contains a `sub1()` method, which performs the subtraction of two numbers. Class C is the class that inherits classes A and B. The `c_obj` instance is an instance of class C. The statement `c_obj.sum1(12,4)` calls the `sum1()` method of class A. The `c_obj.sub1(45,5)` statement calls the `sub1()` method of class B. Let's run the code `classmultiple.py`:

Output of program classmultiple.py

The preceding output shows that the program is running successfully.

Multilevel inheritance

In this type of inheritance, a class can inherit from a child class or derived class. Let's take a simple example code `classmultilevel.py` to understand:

```
class A():
  def sum1(self,a,b):
    c = a+b
    return c

class B(A):
  pass

class C(B):
  pass

c_obj = C()
print "Sum is ", c_obj.sum1(12,4)
```

In the preceding example, you can see that class B inherited from class A and class C inherited from class B. The instance of class C can call the method of class A. Let's see the output:

Output of code classmultilevel.py

The preceding output shows that the code is running successfully.

Overriding methods

Overriding the methods allows a user to override the parent class method. Sometimes the class provides a generic method, but in the child class, the user wants a specific implementation of the method. The name of the method must be the same in the parent class and the child class.

Let's see the program `classover1.py`:

```
class A():
  def sum1(self,a,b):
    print "In class A"
    c = a+b
    return c

class B(A):
  def sum1(self,a,b):
    print "In class B"
    c= a*a+b*b
    return c

b_obj = B()
print B.__dict__
print b_obj.sum1(4,5)
```

In the preceding example, classes A and B both have the same method `sum1()` with different implementations. We also have printed the class name space using `B.__dict__`. Let's see the output of the code:

```
C:\Windows\System32\cmd.exe

F:\project_7days\class>python classover1.py
{'__module__': '__main__', '__doc__': None, 'sum1': <function sum1 at 0x00000000
02665A58>, 'f': 7}
In class B
41

F:\project_7days\class>
```

Output of code classover1.py

In the preceding output, you can see the `sum1` function. The Interpreter first checks the instance's class name space: if the method is found, the interpreter uses it.

Operator overloading

In this section, we will learn about operator overloading with special methods. Generally, people call them magic methods. We will use these methods in operator overloading. First, let's understand what operator overloading is.

Using a special method, we'll able to change the built-in behavior of the operator. The special method is surrounded by double underscores (__). Some people called it the dunder method. Let's take an example of the + operator, as shown in the following example:

```
>>> "M"+"R"
'MR'
>>> 4+6
10
>>>
```

You can see a different behavior of the + operator. The integer number is added and the strings are concatenated. Depending upon the object you are working with, the + operator has different behavior. However, the + calling is a special method that runs in the background. In order to do addition of two integers, the + operator calls int.__add__(1,2) and for string addition + calls str.__add__("a", "b"). Refer to the following example:

```
>>> int.__add__(4,6)
10
>>> str.__add__("M","R")
'MR'
>>>
```

So we can customize the addition using the __add__() method. Let's take an example of the following code classoperator1.py, which is very much similar to the earlier code snippets:

```
class Leapx_org():
    def __init__(self,first,last,pay):
        self.f_name = first
        self.l_name = last
        self.pay_amt = pay
        self.full_name = first+" "+last

    def make_email(self):
        return self.f_name+ "."+self.l_name+"@xyz.com"

L_obj1 = Leapx_org('mohit', 'RAJ', 60000)
L_obj2 = Leapx_org('Ravender', 'Dahiya',70000)
print L_obj1+L_obj2
```

We will add two instances L_obj1 and L_obj2. Let's see the output:

Output of code classoperator1.py

The preceding output shows an error in the code. Error for the + operator L_obj1 and L_obj2 are unsupported. We don't know what we want to get from the addition. Consider we want to add the pay amount of both the instances. When I use obj1+L_obj2, the + operator should add the pay amount, which means *60000+70000*. Let's refer to the program and see how to overload the + operator:

```
class Leapx_org():
    def __init__(self,first,last,pay):
        self.f_name = first
        self.l_name = last
        self.pay_amt = pay
        self.full_name = first+" "+last

    def make_email(self):
        return self.f_name+ "."+self.l_name+"@xyz.com"

    def __add__(self,other):
        result = self.pay_amt+ other.pay_amt
        return result
L_obj1 = Leapx_org('mohit', 'RAJ', 60000)
L_obj2 = Leapx_org('Ravender', 'Dahiya',70000)
print L_obj1+L_obj2
```

The preceding program is the same as the previous one except for the magic __add__() method. When we use L_obj1+L_obj2, then the + operator calls the __add__() method. The __add__() method accepts two instances as arguments. The syntax result = self.pay_amt+ other.pay_amt signifies the addition of pay_amt of two instances, which are L_obj1 and L_obj2, in our case. Let's see the output:

Output of classoperator2.py

Let's do one more program, which compares `pay_amt` for both the instances. Here is the code for `classoperator3.py`:

```
class Leapx_org():
    def __init__(self,first,last,pay):
        self.f_name = first
        self.l_name = last
        self.pay_amt = pay
        self.full_name = first+" "+last

    def make_email(self):
        return self.f_name+ "."+self.l_name+"@xyz.com"

    def __gt__(self,other):
        return self.pay_amt>=other.pay_amt

L_obj1 = Leapx_org('mohit', 'RAJ',60000)
L_obj2 = Leapx_org('Ravender', 'Dahiya',70000)
print L_obj1>L_obj2
```

In the preceding program, the last statement `L_obj1>L_obj2` would call the `__gt__()` method which accepts two instances; in this method, we perform a comparison based on their `pay_amt`. Let's see the output:

Output of program classoperator3.py

Do your experiment with different `pay_amt` values.

Let's use the same program and print the instance length and instance. Refer to the code for `classoperator4.py`:

```
class Leapx_org():
    def __init__(self,first,last,pay):
        self.f_name = first
        self.l_name = last
        self.pay_amt = pay
        self.full_name = first+" "+last

    def make_email(self):
        return self.f_name+ "."+self.l_name+"@xyz.com"

L_obj1 = Leapx_org('mohit', 'RAJ',60000)
print L_obj1
print "n"
print "Lenght is ",len(L_obj1)
```

In the preceding code, we have printed the instance and length of the instance. Let's see the output:

Output of code classoperator4.py

We need to use two magic methods: to customize the instance print, we will use `__str__()` and to find out the length, we will use `__len__()`. For the `__len__()` method, we will use the length of the full name. See the code `classoperator5.py`:

```
class Leapx_org():
    def __init__(self,first,last,pay):
        self.f_name = first
        self.l_name = last
        self.pay_amt = pay
        self.full_name = first+" "+last
```

```
    def make_email(self):
        return self.f_name+ "."+self.l_name+"@xyz.com"

    def __str__(self):
        str1 = "instance belongs to "+self.full_name
        return str1

    def __len__(self):
        return len(self.f_name+self.l_name)
L_obj1 = Leapx_org('mohit', 'RAJ',60000)
print L_obj1
print "n"
print "Lenght is ",len(L_obj1)
```

As discussed earlier, we need to use two methods: one is __str__() and the second one is __len__(). We used the customize output instance is belong to. The __len__() function returns the combined length of the first name and the second name. Refer to the output:

Output of code classoperator5.py

Bingo! So both our purposes are served, the customized output and the length of the instance are being printed. I hope you got an idea how to use operator overloading and magic methods.

The class method

You have seen the regular class methods of the class. The regular method automatically takes an instance as the first argument, and, by convention, we called it self. How can we pass the class as an argument so that we can change the class variable in the method? To do that, we use the class method.

The class method takes the class as first argument. To turn the regular method into the class method, we will use decorator (@classmethod) at the top of the method. Let's see the methodclass1.py example:

```
class Leapx_org():
    mul_num = 1.20
    def __init__(self,first,last,pay):
        self.f_name = first
        self.l_name = last
        self.pay_amt = pay
        self.full_name = first+" "+last

    def make_email(self):
        return self.f_name+ "."+self.l_name+"@xyz.com"

    def incrementpay(self):
        self.pay_amt = int(self.pay_amt*self.mul_num)
        return self.pay_amt

    @classmethod
    def mul_num_set(cls, amt):
        cls.mul_num=amt

L_obj1 = Leapx_org('mohit', 'RAJ', 60000)
L_obj2 = Leapx_org('Ravender', 'Dahiya',70000)
Leapx_org.mul_num_set(1.40)
print L_obj1.mul_num
print L_obj2.mul_num
```

In the preceding program, a couple of things are new. The regular method mul_num_set() has been converted into the class method using the decorator @classmethod at the top. In the mul_num_set(cls,amt) method, the first argument cls represents the class. By convention, we are using cls. Don't use class as the argument because class is the keyword, use it to define a class. The syntax cls.mul_num=amt sets the mul_num class variable to the amt value, which is passed by the line Leapx_org.mul_num_set(1.40). The line Leapx_org.mul_num_set(1.40) calls the class method mul_num_set() using the class. You can also use an instance to call the class method as shown in L_obj1.mul_num_set(1.40):

Let's run the program:

Output of program methodclass1.py

The same thing can be achieved using the `Leapx_org.mul_num= 1.40` line. But here we used the class method.

The static method

The static method doesn't take an instance or class as the first argument. They are just simple functions. But we include them in class because they have some logical connection with the class. Consider a situation in the `methodclass1.py` program, when the pay of a person is less than `50000`, then the incremented pay amount would be `1.30`of pay amount , otherwise `1.20`. To turn a regular method into a class method, we will use decorator (`@staticmethod`) at the top of the method.

Let's make the program:

```
class Leapx_org():
    mul_num = 1.20
    mul_num2 = 1.30
    def __init__(self,first,last,pay):
        self.f_name = first
        self.l_name = last
        self.pay_amt = pay
        self.full_name = first+" "+last
    @staticmethod
    def check_amt(amt):
        if amt <50000:
            return True
        else :
            return False
    def incrementpay(self):
        if self.check_amt(self.pay_amt):
            self.pay_amt = int(self.pay_amt*self.mul_num2)
```

```
        else :
            self.pay_amt = int(self.pay_amt*self.mul_num)
            return self.pay_amt

L_obj1 = Leapx_org('mohit', 'RAJ', 40000)
L_obj2 = Leapx_org('Ravender', 'Dahiya',70000)
L_obj1.incrementpay()
L_obj2.incrementpay()
print L_obj1.pay_amt
print L_obj2.pay_amt
```

In the preceding program, the check_amt() method is a static method as specified by the decorator @staticmethod. The check_amt() method checks whether amt is greater than 50000 or not. The incrementpay() method uses the check_amt() static method. The check_amt() method does not change the class and instance variable. But it has some logical connection with regular method incrementpay().

Refer to the following output:

Output of program staticmethod1.py

Hope you understood the static method.

The private variable

Python doesn't have real private methods, so two underlines at the beginning make a variable and a method private. Let's see a very simple example:

```
class A:
    __amount = 45
    def __info(self):
        print "I am in Class A"
    def hello(self):
        print "Amount is ",A.__amount
```

```
a = A()
a.hello()
a.__info()
a.__amount
```

In the preceding program, __info() is the private method and __amount is the private variable. Let's see the output:

Output of program private1.py

You can see the benefit of the private variable. Outside the class, you cannot access the private method as well as the private variable, but inside the class, you can access the private variables. In the hello() method, the __amount variable can be accessed as shown in the output (Amount is printed).

However, you can access private variables and the private method from outside the class. Use the syntax like instance _class-name__private-attribute.

Now, let's rewrite the program with the correct syntax:

```
class A:
    __amount = 45

    def __info(self):
        print "I am in Class A"

    def hello(self):
        print "Amount is ",A.__amount

a = A()
a.hello()
a._A__info()
print a._A__amount
```

Let's see the output:

Output of program private1.py

So what is the benefit of accessing private variable outside the class. The benefit is to prevent the class method and variable being changed by others accidentally. Hope you get the idea of private methods.

Summary

In this chapter, we have learned what is class and the benefits of creating a class.
We learned how to create an instance or an object. Instance and object are the same thing.
We learned the difference between class variable and instance variable. Class variables are shareable among all the regular methods. Static methods are unique to instances. In class inheritance, we learned the benefit of inheritance and code reuse. By using method overriding, we can override the method of the parent class. In operator overloading, we learned how to change the behavior of the built-in operator. We learned why to create static and class methods. The class methods are created to change class attributes. In the end, we learned the benefits of private methods and private variables.

Index

www.ingramcontent.com/pod-product-compliance
Lightning Source LLC
Chambersburg PA
CBHW060527060326
40690CB00017B/3406